Crowned

Gender Equality + The Gospel

———

Kelly Symone

Dedication

"Go and tell my daughters they have already been crowned."

This book was written in response to God's instruction to me in November 2015. It has been my honor and my privilege to chronicle God's heart for us and publish it for all to read. I pray that all who find this book would fall deeper in love with our just and compassionate God whose Words are life and instruction.

May the power of God meet you in these pages to change your mind and transform our world.

The Lord gives the word; the women who announce the news are a great host.
Psalm 68:11

Table of Contents

Introduction

The Daughters Have a Name

We know Job's story.

An incredibly wealthy, God-fearing, family man had everything in the world going for him until it all came crashing down. In one of the worst plot twists you could imagine, Job loses all of his flocks, his servants, all of his children and contracts some horrible sickness that leaves him with boils all over his body. But Job never loses his reverence for God. This is remarkable considering that most of his friends and his wife had nothing good to say about Job or God at that point. Job wouldn't turn his back on God. Eventually, things turned around for him and he was restored to a better state than he was in before all his troubles started. The book of Job ends with him accumulating greater wealth, having a second set of children and his good health restored. It's a satisfying end to a weird, tumultuous story. But Job wasn't the only one who was better off, after all was said and done.

Job's first group of children had him constantly in prayer. We don't learn any of their names in the text, but maybe they were a bit rowdy and worrisome to Job. But something was different about Job's second group of children. The Bible gives the names of the daughters but not the sons. I hear God saying now that his daughters have a name.

The Prophecy

We are in a time when God is restoring the name, the beauty and the wealth of his daughters. These women will not be nameless, faceless or forgotten. They have been recorded and remembered. Yes, God's daughters have their own names and their own identities. They are distinguished and not dependent upon the names of any men for significance or fame. No, God has identified his daughters and is exposing them through their beauty. The beauty of God's daughters is world-renowned. It will not be a secret and it cannot be hidden. God has arranged it all from the beginning and has chosen now to be the time of revealing. For it is the women who carry double glory-

—the women are the glory of men, and the men are the glory of God (1 Corinthians 11:7).

This is the time of God's beauty being exposed through the daughters. God is making himself very clear and explaining precisely who he is through the daughters. And all of the glory is for God. The beauty is a reflection of the light of God's glory. And the women will have wealth. God's daughters have their own inheritance and it is not dependent upon whom they marry. They have an inheritance that comes with their identity. This inheritance is not a slap in the face or a challenge to their brothers. God's sons have an inheritance alongside their sisters. Yes, God's sons and daughters are on equal standing in the spirit and on the earth. This is what God is explaining now.

The Revelation

When God restored Job, the daughters were elevated. This is the time we are entering now. This is a time for the daughters to be elevated to our rightful place and obtain our inheritance alongside our brothers.

Each of Job's daughters was named to mark the season of suffering coming to an end—Jemima, which means 'Daylight'; Kezia, which means 'It is done'; and, Kerenhappuch which symbolizes a cosmetic for women's eyes and also means 'to shine.' Yes, the daughters are not only beautiful, but we are beautifiers coming to set in order what was in disarray, to make lovely, to artfully arrange and create pleasantness according to the standard of the Most High God. No other standard is relevant or will endure. True beauty, internal and external, will always reflect the light of the Son. Be courageous and rejoice! Daylight has come, the suffering is done and now it is time to shine!

Sounds awesome! But now what? How do we actually become who God has always intended us to become? To understand our identity, we have to go back to the beginning of life, as we know it. Usually, when people talk about the creation story, we tend to stick to the high-level details:

Once upon a time, there was God and nothing else. But then God said. And all the earth, water, plants, and animals showed up. Then God said we should have people. So now there are people, too. But we kind of messed it all up, listening to a snake in the grass. Long story short, we got kicked out of the best place ever and we've been trying to get back ever since. That about sums it up, right?

Well, maybe some details deserve a closer look.

What It Means To Be Human

Let's go to the book of Genesis.

Imagine...nothingness. That's right, just enough substance to make out that there was once something here but not enough to be able to distinguish shapes or forms. All that can be seen is emptiness and pointlessness. And in the midst of all that lifelessness, God speaks. Why did God speak? Because God is fruitful and the expanse before him did not agree with his character. So he changed it to something he could get behind and give meaning. This is so important because if you don't understand this, you won't get anything else in this book: All of creation is a response to God's identity. All creation is God-sourced and proof that God exists. That means that every blade of grass, ocean wave, tiger's paw, and human being was created to identify God as our source and creator. When you understand this underlying reason for being, you realize why it's impossible to know your specific purpose without direct engagement of your Creator. You are in danger of wasting your time if you ask another person to identify your purpose or expect your relationships with others to fulfill you completely. Only God is qualified to tell you why you were born.

In the first chapter of Genesis, we see that the earth had no shape and no function. There was no sign of life, except for God's spirit hovering above the waters. Then all of a sudden, God, the inventor of language, utters the words that changed nothing into something, "Light, be!" As God continued to speak, the earth continued to develop substance into sustenance and spark the elements into forming rushing seas, sparkling stars, vast oceans, lush fields and amazingly unique birds and animals to populate the planet. Isn't the power contained in God's words amazing?

Now when God created human beings, the pattern changed a little bit. Instead of just saying something like, "People, be!", God says this:

> "Let us make man in our image, after our likeness. And let them have dominion over the fish of the sea and over the birds of the heavens and over the livestock and over all the earth and over every creeping thing that creeps on the earth."
>
> Genesis (*English Standard Version* 1:26)

Did you notice that God was talking to God?

Yes, that's right. When God created humanity, God created a mirror image being destined to act like and look like God. Depending upon what you may have heard or been taught in the past, this may be a hard concept to grasp at first. There are so many differences of opinion about the value of human lives.

Some people think that life and value begin at conception, while others believe that life begins at birth. Some people only value the lives of people who look like them or think like them or believe in the same god. But if we evaluate our worth from how we were created and who we were created to look like, I submit that God established the value of a human at the beginning of life on earth. Doesn't it make sense that the maker and creator of something would be the expert and determiner of its worth and value?

When God decided to create us, it wasn't good enough to speak, "Be!" into the atmosphere. God had to look to God's own image as the source and very substance from which we take shape. We are the only creation that God commanded out of God's own Spirit. We are spirit-beings created by a Spirit-being (John 4:24). Let's go to the next verse:

> So God created man in his own image, in the image of God he created him; male and female he created them.
>
> Genesis 1:27

We're going to do a little bit of digging here. Not one book of the Bible was written in the English language, and some of the true meaning of the words are lost in translation. The Old Testament or Hebrew Bible was predominately written in the Hebrew language, and Hebrew can have several words that can translate to one English word. The Hebrew word variations carry subtle and not-so-subtle differences in meaning that bring a deeper level of understanding to the writer's message. In this case, the Hebrew word *bara* was translated as 'created' in verse 27. When you study the word *bara* in Hebrew, you find that one of its meanings is to 'fashion by cutting.' When you substitute that phrase for 'created' in verse 27, here's what you get:

> So God fashioned by cutting man in his own image, in the image of God he fashioned by cutting him; male and female he fashioned by cutting them.

Wow! God literally cut us out from God's own Spirit. To be human means to be fashioned by cutting from the image of God.

Let's really make it plain—the word image is defined as a reproduction or imitation of the form of a person or thing[1]. Likeness is defined as resemblance or the quality or state of being like someone or something. The Hebrew word used for image is related to the word idol. An idol was a small statue that represented a god or higher power. That's right—God created us as little idols or representatives of God in the earth. In other words, we were created to look and act like God here on earth. When you understand how you were created, you will never have low self-esteem again. You will never forsake your human dignity again. Look at who you came from— it is truly an honor and privilege to be a human being!

What Is Man?

One thing that sticks out in verse 27 and many other verses that we will examine in this book is the use of the English word 'man.' We have been taught to read 'man' as male, but this is not the intention of the writer of Genesis. The writer used the Hebrew word *haddam* in various forms and this word is defined as mankind. Mankind is another way of saying humanity or humankind, and this term refers to the entire human species. Mankind or *haddam* is not specific to men or women but inclusive of both men and women. This is a tremendously vital distinction to make as we continue to build a better understanding of what happened to humanity in the book of Genesis.

At different points in Genesis, *haddam* is translated as Adam. We recognize Adam to be a proper noun or the name of a specific person: in this case, the first male human to live on earth. The translators used the proper name Adam solely to refer to the male human, but the writer of Genesis does not make this distinction. In truth, the author states that God called their name *haddam* meaning that God referred to both man and woman together as humankind (Genesis 5:2). There are different Hebrew words used to refer to male humans and female humans, and the author uses each of them when appropriate. In the book of John, we learn that God is the Word (John 1:1). If God is the Word, then it's safe to assume that God invented language and understands how to skillfully and intentionally use words to communicate. With that being said, there's no point in putting words in God's mouth. God is quite capable of speaking God's own mind. If God intended to call out men or women specifically, then the author would have written it that way. But that's just not how it was written. Keep this in mind when you are reading through the verses referenced in this section and when you read the Bible in your study time. God knows how to talk.

In truth, nowhere in the text do we see God was making any distinction in value, dignity, or authority between male and female humans. As far as God is concerned, male and female humans are equal in weight and equal in dignity. Since God is the original substance of both male and female, there actually can't be any disparity or inequity between them. If there were a disparity, then that would mean that one of them came from a different source. In fact, what gives both male and female their value is their source.

Men and women are equal because God is our point of origin. So God created male and female from God's own image and then gave them a job and some instructions:

> And God blessed them. And God said to them, "Be fruitful and multiply and fill the earth and subdue it, and have dominion over the fish of the sea and over the birds of the heavens and over every living thing that moves on the earth." And God said, "Behold I have given you every plant yielding seed that is on the face of all the earth, and every tree with seed in its fruit. You shall have them for food. And to every beast of the earth and to every bird of the heavens and to everything that creeps on the earth, everything that has the breath of life, I have given every green plant for food. And it was so. Genesis 1:28-30

Reading these verses, we see that God gave male and female the responsibility of taking care of the earth, multiplying what had been created, and reigning over all of God's creation on earth. God is essentially putting them in charge of bringing order. Then God explained what they should use as food for themselves and the rest of creation. At this point in scripture, we are only discussing male and female in spirit form. We have not gotten to the point of discussing male human beings (men) and female human beings (women) because humanity has not yet appeared in physical form. Not a plant or animal had yet appeared in its physical form. Genesis 2 is where we start to see the physical appearance of everything God created in chapter 1.

The Making of Mankind

Take a look at our next passage:

> When no bush of the field was yet in the land and no small plant of the field had yet sprung up– for the LORD God had not caused it to rain in the land, and there was no man(kind) to work the ground, and a mist was going up from the land and was watering the face of the whole ground– then the LORD God formed the man(kind) of dust from the ground and breathed into his nostrils the breath of life, and the

man(kind) became a living creature. And the LORD God planted a garden in Eden, in the east, and there he put the man(kind) who he had formed. And out of the ground the LORD God made to spring up every tree that is pleasant to the sight and good for food. The tree of life was in the midst of the garden, and the tree of knowledge of good and evil. Genesis 2:5-9

There is another level of creation taking place in Genesis 2. Again, we see the word form and think nothing unusual was happening here. But here we have another Hebrew word, different from *bara,* that gives a different understanding of how we were made. The original word used for form is *yatsar. Yatsar* means to form like a potter forms clay into a vessel or to carve wood into an image. Essentially, *yatsar* means to squeeze into shape[2]. Humanity was squeezed and molded into shape by God's own hands. After shaping us according to our purpose, then God blew breath into the body and the human became alive. The word used for breath is *neshamah* which is synonymous with spirit. God blew the spirits created in Genesis 1, male and female, into the body that was formed and the body became alive. Let me repeat that. Both of the spirits, male and female, were blown into the nostrils of the first human. To a lot of people, that statement is problematic and suspicious. It goes against what has been taught for centuries in many pulpits. But it's the only way to interpret what the writer is saying throughout the first three chapters of Genesis without adding to his words to fit our typical way of thinking about creation. This doesn't mean that the first human body looked like both sexes. We really don't know what the first human looked like and how the bodies may have changed, especially after God explained the consequences of their disobedience.

As human beings, we tend to think of ourselves as physical beings first and spiritual beings second. We believe what we see, touch, taste, smell, and hear over anything that does not lend itself to being perceived by our physical senses. We're so accustomed to perceiving through our physical senses and experiences, that we use the terms male and female interchangeably with the terms man and woman. But these two sets of words have very different meanings and applications. Male and female are descriptive terms that explain the nature of an existing thing or person. In English grammar, male and female are adjectives that give another dimension of meaning to nouns (people, places, or things). The terms male and female do not exclusively describe human beings. For example, there are male and female animals and parts of plants. Even with electricity, a plug is considered 'male' and an electrical socket is considered 'female.' These are terms that describe something or someone, but they are not the identity of that thing or that person.

We just read that God fashioned by cutting male and female from the Spirit of God. It was God's decision to create male and female to express God on the earth. It was God's decision to make one body first and then another body to house those expressions. Male and female are not just or merely human, because God is not a human being (Numbers 23:19; John 4:24). Male and female are spirit, as God is Spirit.

Man and woman are the spiritual, biological and grammatically correct terms for identifying living human beings. We will dig more into how the Hebrew words for man and woman are introduced into the text in a little while. For now, let's agree that man and woman are nouns that exclusively refer to human beings. They never refer to God, or plants, or animals or any other created thing. So why make all this fuss over separating male and female from man and woman? Because God names people, places, and things according to their respective purposes. When we confuse the names, we confuse the purposes. The purpose of male and female human beings is to, as it says in Genesis 1:28, 'Be fruitful, multiply, fill the earth, subdue it and have dominion.' We will discover the purpose of man and woman as we continue to read through Genesis 2.

Here She Comes

After God formed humankind and gave us life, God put us to work in the garden. When we enter the garden, God gives another set of instructions:

And the LORD God commanded the man(kind),
saying, "You may surely eat of every tree of the
garden, but of the tree of the knowledge of
good and evil you shall not eat, for in the day
that you eat of it you shall surely die."
Genesis 2:16--17

You know when you're watching a movie and the suspenseful music starts playing in the background because something terrible is about to happen? This is that part of our creation story. God's warning about the tree will come back to haunt them later, but for now, let's move on and meet someone special.

Then the LORD God said, "It is not good that
the man(kind) should be alone; I will make a
suitable helper." Now out of the ground LORD
God had formed every beast of the field and
every bird of the heavens and brought them to
the man(kind) to see what they would be called.
And whatever the man(kind) called every living
creature, that was its name. The man(kind)
gave names to all livestock and to the birds of

the heavens and to every beast of the field. But
for man(kind) there was not found a helper fit for
him(humankind).

Genesis 2:18-20 (translated emphasis added)

For the first time in the creation story, we see God saying that something is not good. This statement is a bit of a surprise, considering that God has already finished the work of creation and declared everything to be good in Genesis 1. Why the change of heart? First, let's focus on the word alone. This word is accurately translated from Hebrew, *badad,* but its full meaning is only uncovered by knowing its origin. Did you know that the word alone is a contraction? Any etymological dictionary will tell you that alone is a combination of two Middle English words, all and ane[3]. In Modern English, alone is a contraction of the words all and one, meaning wholly one, unaccompanied or unattended. Some definitions even say that alone means without help. So God is saying that it is not good that the human is all one, wholly one, unaccompanied, unattended or without help. The solution to this problem is to make a 'suitable helper.'

We won't go too far into the meaning of this phrase, but let's briefly discuss the meaning of the word suitable. In Hebrew, the word translated as suitable is *naged*. *Naged* means to appear in front of, opposite to, or in sight of something. So God is making a helper to appear in front of, opposite to, or in view of mankind. It's implied that the helper was there but could not be seen. So then God decides to *yatsar* (form) the animals and birds and bring them to the human to see what they would be called. It seems that God was observing whether or not the human would recognize this 'suitable helper' from the rest of the created living things. But the names that mankind gave them all indicated that none of the animals or birds were suitable. Now let's keep reading to see what happens next:

> So the LORD God caused a deep sleep to fall upon the man(kind), and while he slept took one of the ribs and closed up its place with flesh. And the rib that the LORD God had taken from the man(kind) he made into a woman and brought her to the man(kind). Then man(kind)

said, " This at last is bone of my bones and flesh of my flesh; she shall be called Woman, because she was taken out of Man."
Genesis 2:21-23

After discovering that the suitable helper was not among the animals and birds, mankind took a power nap and underwent some serious spiritual surgery. God took something from mankind to make the woman, but it wasn't a rib. The word *tsela* in Hebrew is translated as 'side' when used outside of the creation story in Genesis. The Septuagint, the ancient Greek translation of the Bible, uses the Greek word *pleura*, which also means 'side of the body.' Also, we see the first mention of the word *ishshah*, which is Hebrew for woman, and the first mention of the word *ish*, which is Hebrew for man. Until this time, we have only read about humankind as a generic human being housing both the male and female spiritual expressions of God. Now we are meeting humankind as man and woman, a single species containing the male and female expressions of God in two bodies instead of one. Once again, we see God in the process of making something. The word make here is yet another Hebrew word, *banah*, meaning 'to build.' Considering that God is using pre-existing, pre-formed material from the human, it makes sense that God would have to construct a woman and not just form her. My pastor likes to joke that *banah* is the Bible's way of saying that the woman was "built" or a "brick house."

There are a few things to pay attention to when reading through this passage. God makes the woman but doesn't blow the breath of life into her nostrils. Remember when God formed and breathed into mankind's body? Did you notice that God only breathed into the nostrils once? God did not see the need to repeat that exact process. Simply put, it's not necessary to breathe life into someone that is already alive. The reality that God didn't blow into her nostrils further illustrates that the first human being contained both the male and female spirits. The living female spirit was built into the woman's body once God constructed her from mankind's side.

It is mankind, not the man alone, that recognizes and calls her Woman. In Hebrew, the 23rd verse contains the words *haddam*, *ishshah*, and *ish* to give a precise account of what was happening and who was speaking during this momentous occasion. When we read the verse as it is written, we see that humankind (now man and woman) made the statement in unison. Therefore, the man did not name the woman. Humankind collectively identified themselves as man and woman, finishing their joint work of naming all of God's creation.

Mankind was created (*bara*) and made (*yatsar*) outside of the garden in Eden. The woman was built (*banah*) inside of the garden in Eden. Where the woman was created is a clue to her purpose. The conditions of the garden in Eden were not the same conditions as the rest of the earth. How do we know? We can tell by reading through Genesis 2:8-15 that mankind was responsible for cultivating and overseeing the garden in Eden. God only saw fit to make the female human visible once mankind was placed in the garden. She was conceived of the spirit outside the garden, but she was born in Eden. Eden means delight or pleasure in Hebrew. The woman was born in the place of God's delight, surrounded by every pleasant tree and fruit in a garden irrigated by rivers that flowed in every direction. She was born in the place of purpose and surrounded by pleasure. The rest of the earth, however, was not so lovely. Back in Genesis 1:28, God charges male and female with the responsibility of being fruitful, multiplying and filling the earth, subduing it and having dominion over it and all of God's creation on earth.

After they announce themselves as man and woman, the writer makes a game-changing statement that we will talk about throughout the rest of this book.

> Therefore a man shall leave his father and his mother and hold fast to his wife, and they shall become one flesh. And the mankind and his wife were both **naked** and were not ashamed. Now the serpent was more **crafty** than any other beast of the field that the LORD God had made.

There is a little play on words happening here. *Arumim* is translated as naked when referring to our human ancestors. This nakedness is usually taken literally, but it also applies to the depth of their intimacy. There was nothing hidden between them and there was complete trust. *Arum*, however, is translated as crafty when referring to the serpent. Though the two words are very similar in appearance, they couldn't be more different in meaning. The snake certainly had a hidden agenda and was not trustworthy at all. The Bible also talks about the man and woman being unashamed. Shame is defined as a painful feeling of humiliation or distress caused by the consciousness of wrong or foolish behavior. Without getting too technical, Hebrew uses different verb tenses and voices to indicate how you should interpret the meaning of a sentence. The use of shame in verse 25 is reflexive and imperfect, which tells us that this statement is about how they continuously felt about themselves. Two antonyms, or opposites, for the word shame are glory and honor[4]. In summary, mankind and woman were both uncovered and feeling no sense of humiliation or regret about themselves. They were "dressed" in glory and honor. That's a far cry from merely walking around the garden without any clothes!

We've come a long way in painting a picture of how the creation story happened according to how it is written in the original text. Through the imagery presented by the writer, we see that God thought very highly of humanity, both male and female. The honor of being the only creation that is sourced from God's Spirit just cannot be overstated. God gave humanity, in spirit form, the privilege and responsibility of carrying God's image and likeness on the earth through the positions of caretaker and ruler over all of God's earthly creations. Then we discovered the process of creating humanity started by fashioning us out of God's spirit, molding dust into the shape of a single person, and then building a second person out of the first, leaving us with the uniquely human identities of male-man and female-woman. Man and woman serve as physical representations of the male and female human spirit on the earth and carry the inherent dignity, value, and equality sourced from the Spirit that created us. Finally, we now understand that human beings lived in the garden in an uncovered state of glory and honor that made it impossible for them to feel ashamed of themselves. Everything was great and it seems we were living the dream. So how did we get from there to here?

The End of the Beginning

I'm not a huge fan of scary movies, mostly because I find them funny instead of frightful. But I will admit to feeling a sense of impending doom when one of the characters inevitably heads down some dark, shadowy hallway or trips and falls running away from the bad guy. I've even yelled at the screen, saying,"Don't open that door!" or something like that, as if the clueless victim could hear me. Well, we've come to that part of our story: this is when you clutch your pearls, throw up your hands in disgust, or hide your face because you know somebody's about to make some bad decisions.

We already know that the serpent was the wisest beast in the field (Genesis 3:1). We don't know why the serpent allowed itself to be used for such an evil purpose, considering it was supposed to be under the authority of the humans. Now the serpent was set on uncovering the truth in a different way than the unashamed humans had come to live their lives. The serpent's intentions were nefarious. Let's see what it said:

> He said to the woman, "Did God actually say, 'You shall not eat of any tree of the garden'?" And the woman said to the serpent, "We may eat of the fruit of the trees in the garden, but God said, 'You shall not eat of the fruit of the tree in the midst of the garden, neither shall you touch it, lest you die." But the serpent said to the woman, "You will not surely die. For God knows that when you eat of it your eyes will be opened, and you will be like God, knowing good and evil." So when the woman saw that the tree was good for food, and that it was a delight to the eyes, and that the tree was to be desired to

make one wise, she took of its fruit and ate, and she also gave some to her husband who was with her, and he ate. Then the eyes of both were opened, and they knew they were naked. And they sewed fig leaves together and made themselves loincloths.

Genesis 3:2-7

There are a few alarms that should go off after reading this conversation. The serpent approaches the woman and directs all of its questions to her alone. This is another major key to unlocking the woman's purpose. Much has been said about whose sin caused all of humanity to cut ties with God. Some have interpreted Romans 5:17 to state that once Adam (by himself) ate the fruit, all of humanity lost our relationship with God. To explain the scriptures in that way, you would have to read Adam as only our male human ancestor's name. But we already know that, from God's perspective, Adam refers to humankind (Genesis 5:2) and not a specific man. If we interpreted that scripture as applying only to the man, we would deny the woman's culpability for disobeying God's command.

We already know that both man and woman, male and female, were both equal in responsibility. So it makes sense that they would be equal in blame. But the question remains—what made the serpent target the woman?

In Isaiah, we learn that satan was originally an angel named Lucifer who too highly esteemed himself and sought to replace God on the throne (Isaiah 14:12-17; Revelation 12:9-10). You could say that Lucifer sought God's glory and wanted to be worshipped. In fact, the devil tempted Jesus in the wilderness by offering him the glory of the kingdoms of the world in exchange for his worship (Matthew 4:8-11). Even then, the devil was after Jesus' glory and worship. The woman was taken out of mankind in the garden to be in a body of her own. She emerges in the luxurious place of God's glory on earth. It is no accident ,then, that Paul later states that woman is the glory of man. For the woman is the last of God's creation and carries both the glory of God and mankind (1 Corinthians 11:7). Another way of understanding glory is to think of what gives someone or something weight or esteem or prominence. When an athlete wins a contest, they are highly esteemed or glorified. David calls God the King of glory in Psalm 24:10, because of God's strength in battle and position as owner of the earth. Now is it clear why the serpent targeted the woman? What better way to insult God than by attacking God's most prized creation—humankind? And what is more strategic than targeting the glory of God's most prized creation—woman? It's a two-for-one deal.

Let's go back to Genesis 3. Did you notice that the woman incorrectly answers the serpent's question? God never said that they couldn't touch the tree. It seems harmless that she added this part, but this small addition is what convinced the serpent that it could deceive her. What exactly does it mean to deceive someone? Let's do another word study. Deceive is a compound word made from the prefix de- and the Latin root word -cept. The prefix de- is often refers to something moving down or away or becoming undone, like in the word detach. The root word -cept means "taken," like in the word accept. When you put the two together, you get the word deceive which essentially means to remove or take something away from someone. In the case of the serpent and the woman, it was the truth that was "taken away." It's not that the truth was never known because that would mean she was ignorant of what God said. The Bible tells us that to know the right thing to do and refuse to do it is sin (James 4:17). She should not have allowed herself to be taken away from the truth. If she had remained in the truth, the serpent would not have been able to successfully convince her to eat the fruit.

It's hard to see how she got it so wrong unless you have lived through enough hard times to understand how easy it is to forget or misunderstand what God has said to you. Remember when we talked about how mankind originally housed both male and female before the woman's body was made? That means that she heard when God said "let us create mankind in our own image and likeness..." back in the first chapter of Genesis. Now if God said that you were created in the image and likeness of God, why would you think that a piece of fruit could give you something that you already had? Right here is where we see a pattern of thinking that many women fall into today—seeking validation from an outside source instead of from God. When God tells you who you are, the matter is settled. Thinking that she was less than what God said is why she failed to subdue and have dominion over the serpent, as was her birthright and responsibility.

Once they had eaten from the forbidden tree, they suddenly realized that they were naked. The glory was gone and now they felt exposed. Trusting in their own desires resulted in them stepping outside of what was good into what God said was not good for them. And now they were naked and ashamed. They went from having perfect intimacy to feeling like they needed to protect themselves. So they tried to cover themselves with fig leaves, but those leaves paled in comparison to the glory that once covered them. Everything we do to add to ourselves always ends up looking like a cheap imitation of God's glory.

It All Falls Down

When God enters the scene, the conversation conveys the depths to which humanity has fallen away from perfect relationship with God and each other. Instead of being unified as God had designed, humankind was now blaming each other for their predicament. After listening to their excuses, God explains the consequences to the serpent, the woman, and the man. To the serpent, God said,

> "Because you have done this, cursed are you above all livestock and above all beasts of the field; on your belly you shall go, and dust you shall eat all the days of your life. I will put enmity between you and the woman, and between your seed and her seed; he shall bruise your head, and you shall bruise his heel."
> Genesis 3:14-15

Here we see God setting the stage for a war between the serpent and the woman. It's a war that humanity ultimately wins, but God is telling us that there will be pain. Many would look to this passage as a prophecy pointing specifically to Jesus. While it is true that God is foretelling Jesus' arrival and victory, all of us that follow Jesus are included in this passage. God is predicting Jesus' victory and our victory in him. Our victory is a lifestyle, not an event. To the woman, God said:

> "I will surely multiply your pain in childbearing; in pain you shall bring forth children. Your desire shall be contrary to your husband, but he shall rule over you."
>
> Genesis 3:16

This passage explains the consequence of the woman's disobedience to God. Contrary to popular opinion, God did not curse her. God explains to her that childbearing will now be painful and the dynamic between her and her husband would change. Instead of being treated as an equal, she (and every woman afterward) would have an overwhelming desire for her husband but he would dominate her. It should be noted that this is a negative consequence to her disobedience and not the way God originally designed the husband-wife relationship. If God had intended for men to rule over women or husbands to rule over wives, then this passage would not make much sense. It would just be affirming the current state of their relationship, instead of explaining a radical shift. Finally, to the man/humankind, God said:

> "Because you have listened to the voice of your wife and have eaten of the tree of which I commanded you, 'You shall not eat of it,' cursed is the ground because of you; in pain you shall eat of it all the days of your life; thorns and thistles it shall bring forth for you; and you shall eat the plants of the field. By the sweat of your face you shall eat bread, till you return to the ground, for you are dust, and to dust you shall return."
> Genesis 3:17-19

There are two ways to read this passage. You can read this as God addressing the man by himself or as God addressing humanity, man and woman included. The implications are undoubtedly valid for men and women. Toil, sweat, pain, and death are not gender exclusive. After God has explained all of these things, we now see that the man and woman go by different names. This is the first time in Genesis that the woman is identified separately from the man by name. Naming the woman Eve, or Havah in Hebrew, is the beginning of the fulfillment of God's saying to them that she would be ruled by her husband. In God's eyes, however, her name is Adam.

> This is the book of the generations of Adam. When God created man, he made him in the likeness of God. Male and female he created them, and he blessed them and named them Man (*haddam*) when they were created.
> Genesis 5:1-2

In fact, nowhere in the Bible will you see God refer to the woman as Eve. As far as God is concerned, they were one and remain one. This is an essential key to understanding the concept of the first Adam and the last Adam. Just as the woman was included in God's creation, command and chastisement of Adam, we are included in the death, resurrection, and rulership of Jesus as his bride as the last Adam. We'll dig more into that in a bit. For now, let's recap what we know about the human identity:

1. To be human means to be made in the image and likeness of God. We are designed to imitate and look like God here on earth. When we are not acting like God, we are not acting "human."

2. Male and female human beings are equally created in the image and likeness of God. Male and female are two expressions of the same Spirit, manifested in our human bodies as man and woman. Our point of origin is what makes us equal.

3. The woman was not built from a rib but emerges from the side of the first human being. Her spirit, female, was housed in the first human and now has its own body, called Woman.

4. Man and woman had perfect relationship with each other and with God. This is why the writer describes them as "naked and unashamed." They had no hidden

agendas and were completely transparent with each other and with God.

5. After the man and woman decided to trust their own desires instead of God, God explained the consequences of their actions. One of those consequences was the disruption of the man--woman dynamic of equality, which resulted in the woman being dominated by the man. This was not God's original design.

Now that we have a pretty good understanding of the origins of humanity, let's focus on the purpose of the woman.

The Recipe

Our society has a lot to say about women. From magazines to commercials to fashion labels to talk shows, opinions on women span widely and run strong. Throughout history, society has tried to answer the woman question many times. It seems like every 25 years, there's a new way of understanding the identity and role of women in our culture.

Should a woman be educated? Should she vote? Should she work outside the home? Should she have a bank account in her own name? Can she be head of a household? Should she choose to raise children on her own? Should she change her name when she gets married? Can she really have it all? While advancements have been made in recognizing a woman's right to vote in elections and have her own money, we still have a long way to go. We have not yet grasped the true identity of the woman. Why? Because we have tried to answer this question without considering God's perspective. Imagine that you decided to cook up a favorite dish for some friends that were over at your house for a visit. While they were busy talking and laughing in your living room, you were at work in the kitchen making a masterpiece. Once everything was perfectly prepared, you called your friends over to see your beautiful, appetizing dish. They enjoyed the meal so much that you barely got to put any on your own plate. As you all were sitting around the table eating, your friends started to wonder how the dish had been made. They started asking themselves questions out loud, trading theories, and, frankly, making up stories about the ingredients and cooking methods. One of your friends browsed through a magazine to see if she could find the recipe, but all she saw was pretty airbrushed pictures, shopping ads, and ten tips for how to prepare a great meal for your man. Another friend opened a book that looked like it would have the answer but only found a bunch of shopping lists full of ingredients for all kinds of recipes. One friend boldly announced that only women could know how to cook your dish and demanded her legal right to know how you did it. Another friend retold a story from his pastor about how men are naturally more logical and better problem-solvers than women, so he figured that he would be the first to figure out the secret to your recipe. Meanwhile, you sat at your table with your mouth wide open, wondering why in the world no one had bothered to just ask you in the first place. This is what we look like to God when we try to figure ourselves out without going back to our Source. Let's not repeat the mistakes of the past. Now is the time to look at ourselves from God's perspective, since no one knows humanity better than our Creator.

What's an Ezer?

Women are God's idea. God's intentions were quite clear when designing women from the start.

And the Lord God said, It is not good that the adam should be alone; I will make him a helper fit for him.

Genesis 2:18

The first description of a woman is a helper fit for or suitable for him (*haddam*). The King James Version of the Bible famously describes the woman as a helpmeet[5]. This unfortunately popular translation is insufficiently equipped to provide the accurate context and depth of meaning imbued within the original language. The original Hebrew words for suitable helper are *ezer kenegdo*. An *ezer kenegdo* is more than a helpmeet—she's a battle partner, an aid in trouble, and a companion that helps to overthrow an adversary. In fact, the Bible records the word *ezer* 21 other times with 19 of those references being made to God. That's right—God is an *ezer*! *Ezer* comes from the root word *azar* and means 'to help or succor.' It's important to be clear about this characterization of help. This kind of help has been characterized as a sustainer[6]. This is not the kind of help that is resigned to picking up socks off the floor, washing dishes and swinging by the dry cleaner's to grab the laundry. This is the kind of help that rescues those in danger, wins victories and saves the day.

In Deuteronomy 33, Jacob's blessing to Judah refers to God as an *ezer*, a help to Judah for his enemies. Jacob's other son, Jeshurun, was blessed to see God riding upon heaven to *ezer* for him. All of Israel regarded God as the shield of its *ezer* - Israel's protector and help in times of trouble. David sang many psalms of God 's *ezer* coming from the sanctuary as support (Psalm 33:30); being an *ezer* and shield (Psalm 33:20); an *ezer* and deliverer (Psalm 70:5).

> I have endowed one who is mighty {a hero, giving him the power to *ezer* - to be a champion for Israel}.
> Psalm 89:19

An *ezer,* in God's eyes, is someone like God— someone who helps to save from destruction or calamity. An *ezer* aids in securing the victory. An *ezer* is a champion. Not one time does the word *ezer* or *azar* refer to someone who is weak, incompetent, less than capable, passive, or inherently subordinate. The word *kenegdo* means to appear conspicuous, to stand in the presence of or to appear before. Essentially, *kenegdo* means to be able to be seen. Another way of putting it is to say that *kenegdo* means counterpart. When you put both words together, *ezer kenegdo* is a champion helper— a counterpart who stands before you to save from destruction and aid in securing the victory. Sounds more like an army buddy than a spouse, right? Notice that the writer of Genesis is not describing the woman in his own words, but quoting what God said about her. In the English language, we set apart what people say with quotation marks. The Hebrew language does not include quotation marks in its grammatical structure, but you can imagine them there whenever you see the writer saying "And God said..." We should always give extra attention to the words that are directly attributed to God. While we know that all scripture is God-inspired, there is always something special when we hear directly from the mouth of the

LORD. God's words are more than inspired–they are life! The life of a woman is found in the mouth of the LORD. We can always bank on the truth of God's words (Numbers 23:19; Hebrews 6:18). Make God's word your filter for anything you hear from anyone before you decide to believe it. If what you hear about women contradicts what God said, consider it a lie and treat it as such. When you hear a lie, decide to believe what God said about the situation. Reject the lie and it will have no choice but to separate itself from you (James 4:7).

From the beginning, the enemy has sought to diminish and warp the identity of human beings as an insult to God. The tactics satan uses to deceive us have not changed. John 10:10 tells us that stealing, killing, and destroying is the enemy's modus operandi. Just as the serpent craftily and cunningly challenged the woman on what God said in the garden, modern-day men and women are confronted daily with pressure to conform to cultural traditions about what it means to be a man or a woman. Most of these ideas are not rooted in God's perspective on humanity. We are made to reflect God's image and likeness, not our own. Yet, the culture inside and outside of church seems to think it can improve upon what God initially had in mind. Let's take a look at some of the lies that currently keep us from living out the identity that God created for us.

Godly Femininity

Godly women are always in demand! The world is waiting for us to come out of hiding and let the light God gave us shine. When we live out of our God-given identities as women, we silently give permission for other women to do the same. It takes courage and strength to be who God created you to be, especially if it does not fit the expectations of others. You will have to change your mind and your habits to reflect the person that God sees when looking at you.

Close your eyes and use your imagination. Imagine that you are viewing millions of men and women living their lives—working, taking care of themselves and their families, and being who they think they are supposed to be. Look to the left of you and you will see a young boy learning what it is to be a man from the multitude of men he witnesses: fathers, brothers, friends, teachers, neighbors, leaders, strangers, and celebrities. As he looks around, he is constantly comparing and contrasting himself against what he sees around him, what seems to be working and what seems to fail, what earns respect and admiration and what ushers in ridicule, what attracts a woman and what repels a woman. When a boy is transitioning into manhood, regardless of sexual orientation, he takes a very definitive view of what he should expect from a woman. He watches women to see how they make decisions, how they feel about themselves, how they dress, how they talk to each other and how they interact with men. What he sees and hears every day is more influential than the fantasies and edited images he sees on TV and the internet. Though TV, film and digital caricatures of women make a powerful impression, what he experiences on a consistent basis is still his primary teacher. As that boy grows into a man, there are several ideas he comes across that may stick in his mind and affect how he sees himself and women:

• Believing that taking care of his own children is akin to "babysitting."

• Desiring to be the sole breadwinner in the home and, subsequently, having final say on all financial decisions.

• Believing that completing domestic chores is "helping" his wife, not part of normal home maintenance for all of the home's residents.

• Desiring a woman to "submit" to him- by being quiet, not offering an alternate point of view for consideration and by yielding unqualified, decision-making to him simply because he is a man.

• Believing that he has a right to have sex with his wife without her permission.

• Believing that it's "natural" for women to work outside the home and also be primarily responsible for most or all domestic and child-rearing responsibilities like cooking, cleaning, grocery- shopping, picking up and dropping off children, keeping up with children's activities and homework, etc.

• Believing that housewives do not work.

• Believing that it is natural for women to make less money than men who do the same work because women are not as productive as men.

• Believing that women are inherently not as good at logical thinking as they are at navigating emotions.

• Believing that women are naturally less qualified for leadership roles at every level, from CEO to governmental positions of authority.

• Believing that a woman's purpose is to help her man fulfill his purpose as if God did not give her a unique purpose assignment of her own.

This list of "natural" or inherent beliefs summarizes in part some of the toxic, misogynistic imaginations that the enemy has used to pollute the minds of billions of men and women throughout history and in modern times. It is past time for us as believers to use the God-given authority given to us by Jesus to cast down these wicked and vain thoughts and ideas that exalt themselves against the knowledge of God. The truth is that it is natural for women to be equal to men in every capacity and context for human existence. Because we are made in the image and likeness of God alongside men, it is natural for women to lead, to nurture, to love, to think, and to act like God. Every negative and demeaning stereotype we attach to a woman, or any other human being, is an affront to their true identity and the Creator who made us. There are many damaging characterizations influencing how we perceive the intrinsic value, purpose and identity of women. Even though these beliefs directly contradict the heart of God and the Word of God, somehow we have allowed these dangerous myths to masquerade as truth and common sense. In doing so, we have subscribed to a double-minded faith—a belief in a God that honors us by making both sexes in the image of God only to demean women by insisting that we are somehow not quite as equally made in that image after all. This is belief mixed with unbelief and God is not at fault here. God's idea of humanity was quite clear from the beginning. We have managed to confuse our traditions for God's intentions. These traditions have handicapped our ability to see God's heart clearly and tainted our collective faith. There are depths of intimacy with God that cannot be reached without corresponding belief. Our walk with the Lord increases in intimacy and depth, with each blessing and each testimony.

You can only impart who you are. You can't give someone something that you don't possess. God is not timid. God is not inferior to anyone or anything. God's intellectual capacity is unmatched. God is not helpless or weak. God leads with excellence and confidence. God makes great decisions. God is never passive or naive. So it is impossible for women to be inherently fearful, inferior, dumb, helpless, weak, passive, chronically insecure or ill-equipped to lead. Every feminine stereotype that demeans women is an attempt by the enemy to confuse our joint-identity with men as God-representatives on the earth. These demonic lies intend to short-circuit the power of all human beings in carrying out our divine responsibilities as co-rulers and custodians of the earth. As long as we are struggling to uncover our true identities and fighting for power with each other, the enemy is free to steal, kill and destroy anything and anyone right under our noses.

We are now standing at the precipice of a new day in which the revelatory light of our identity in Christ has removed the cataracts of insecurity and pride from our eyes. Now we can see how beautiful God made each one of us and how powerful we are when we unite in humility to erase the traces of iniquity from our culture and fulfill the words God spoke into our beings before the foundation of the world. Women and men are meant to lead side by side.

Shared leadership is not a unique concept in the kingdom of God. We consider God the Creator, Jesus and the Holy Spirit to all carry the same identity and authority. We don't play favorites and pick one over the other when we pray. God has chosen to express Himself uniquely as Creator, as Jesus and as Spirit. The diversity in divine expression, however, does not compromise their oneness. Each expression of God is equal in divine glory and authority. If a woman decides to wear a yellow dress to work on Monday, a green sweater to the movies on Tuesday and a white ballgown to a gala on Saturday, does that mean she has switched personalities? Is the ballgown "better" than the sweater? Of course not! She's merely chosen to express herself differently to suit a particular purpose. No matter what outfit she wears, she is still the same person with the same gifts, abilities, and identity she's always had. She only changed her outfit to match the occasion. When God created us, God chose to express himself equally and entirely through male and female human beings. We carry the same image, identity, likeness, responsibilities, and authority. The differences in our packaging and presentation do not change that men and women are cut from the same cloth.

When women step into the identity God has designed for us, all of humanity begins to reflect the image of God into the world the way it was always intended. God gave us an awesome responsibility of being His representatives here on the earth. Without the full participation of women in this noble cause, the enemy has been able to keep the curse in operation in our families, our cities, and throughout the world. It will take the full partnership of men, women and our God to counteract the demonic influence that resulted from our unbelief. We have an opportunity now to gain an understanding of God's original intent for women and be genuinely feminine. Instead of looking to the media or tradition for cues, let's take a look at the Word of God and his character to see the intentions of God's heart for women.

A Godly woman is loved.

It all starts and ends with love. Without love, we are incapable of being our true selves. Without love, we are incapable of believing what God says about us. The apostle John wrote that God is love (1 John 4:8). God doesn't have love; God is the embodiment of love. Love is the defining characteristic of God. Since we are children of the Most High God, it's only right that love would be our defining characteristic, too.

Being loved is the secret ingredient to being a true daughter of God. So many times, women are defined by our relationships with other people—wife, mother, sister, daughter, friend. There is never a shortage of roles for women to fill in the lives of others. While It's rewarding to be so many things to so many people, it's also easy to run out of energy and patience when you have not allowed yourself to be loved first. Every day we need to be intentional in thinking about how much God loves us. Right now, at this very moment, God is singing over you (Zephaniah 3:17). Let God's melody capture your heart and settle your mind that everything God says is right.

Did you know that God has numbered every hair on your head and not one of them will fall to the ground? Did you forget that God promised to never, never, never leave you or turn back on you? Do you recall that Jesus saw your face while he was on the cross and endured the shame to defeat death, sickness, and lack specifically for you? Don't you remember that you are tattooed on God's hands? You cannot be forgotten! (Luke 21:18; Hebrews 13:5; Hebrews 12:2; Isaiah 49:16). Rehearse what God said about you in your mind throughout the day. Jesus tells us to abide in love and to live in God's unconditional, unwavering acceptance and affection for us (John 15; Ephesians 1:6). Sprinting up the ladder of success will not make God love you any more or less. Winning PTA mother of the year will not set you apart in God's eyes. Being the perfect wife will not win you any extra brownie points when it comes to God loving you and approving of you. God decided how to feel about you before you were ever born. There are no merit badges for God's love, so stop trying so hard to win something that's already yours.

All of the power and perspective we need to live our lives well on a daily basis is rooted and grounded in our receptivity and consciousness of God's love in us and for us. A car's job is to move you from place to place. Without gasoline in the tank, a car will not be able to move anywhere and will stay idle on the road. Its purpose and capability will remain the same, but it won't fulfill either one because it doesn't have the right fuel. You and I are the same way. Love is the fuel that enables us to accomplish our God-given purpose. Love is also our filter for how we see the world and how we interact with others. It creates a worldview that empowers us to respond well to every challenge and solve problems for ourselves and others in a way that is consistent with God's heart toward humanity. It is our calling card as Christ-partakers (John 13:35).

When a woman knows that she is loved, she sees herself the way God sees her and not through the media's comparison and anxiety-filled lens. Love takes the pressure off of you to be perfect. Knowing that you are loved allows you to be yourself and feel accepted without demanding that you fit a certain dress size or look a certain way. In fact, love and confidence are a package deal—they always travel together (Galatians 5:6). Love is the no-confidence cure. Instead of trying to work your faith, all you need to do is start with love and it will spark the confidence you need to trust God with managing your life. When you remember how much God loves you, you won't have a problem believing what God says about you.

Sometimes we think too little of the force of love. We relegate it to emotional expression without taking into account that God's love is the genesis for our salvation, our redemption, and our reconciliation back to God. Love is a force and it works! Love is God's method of expansion. Love is how you prepare your heart for God's purpose in your life— growing in love precedes growing in efficacy. It makes room in your heart for God's purpose to be fully expressed.

A Godly woman finds her power in purpose. Everything and everyone God creates has a purpose— a special assignment that gives meaning to life and fulfillment to the one who pursues and accomplishes it. Women were designed with a very specific purpose in mind—to help overthrow an enemy. Godly women are always in pursuit of God-given purpose. Culture and tradition often teach that the most worthy goal of a woman is to be in a relationship with a man and have children. In fact, some very accomplished women feel as though they don't "have it all" until they are married with children. There is no doubt that purpose and relationships are deeply and inextricably connected, but there is subtle idolatry to the belief that the life of a woman is centered on helping others to fulfill their purpose without a specific purpose of her own. The problem with this tradition is that God never said that! In fact, not a single Biblical example of womanhood fits this traditional template. Esther is a great example. Had Esther not been in the Persian palace or had she shied away from the divine opportunity to influence the king, all of her Jewish kin would have been wiped out by genocide. If she were more concerned with pleasing her husband, she would have never risked her life by attempting to save her people. Instead, she seized the moment and demonstrated why she had been "born for such a time as this (Esther 4:14)."

Sarah, Abraham's wife and the first matriarch of the nation of Israel, was significant to God's plan to redeem the human family back to relationship with God. When God assigned Abram to be the father of many nations, God did not call him by himself. In Genesis 17, God changed Abram's name to Abraham to signify the spiritual shift that was taking place in him and us as future believers in Jesus Christ. It was a transformative moment that required Abraham to see himself the way God saw him and for others to change how they engaged him as a result of this shift. But God did not stop at renaming Abram. Sarai was Sarah's original name before God changed it. If it didn't matter how Sarah saw herself and if she had no real significant role to play in the story of God's people, why go through the trouble of changing her name, too? In fact, Sarah was key to God's promise to make their family a blessing to all nations of the earth. The root word that gives the name Sarah its meaning translates to 'ruler,' and the name change reflected that God intended for her and her offspring to rule globally, not just on a local level. It was Sarah's first born child that was the child of promise (Isaac), not Abraham's first child (Ishmael). Later on, Paul reminds the Galatians to act like they are Sarah's children meaning they are freeborn, not slaves like children of the bondwoman Hagar (Galatians 4:21-31). From Abraham, we see a picture of God as our protector and understand how blessing and inheritance works. From Sarah, we realize our identity as free rulers with dominion on the earth. Together, they paint a full picture of how God used both of them in the redemptive plan to get the family of God back in our rightful place.

Godly women know that God calls all of us by name and pours out the Holy Spirit on sons and daughters alike (Isaiah 43:1; Joel 2:28; Acts 2:17). Does it make sense for God to pour out the precious Holy Spirit and call us by name if there were no intent to use us in a specific way? Each of us has the privilege and responsibility of answering that call and making the most of whatever God has given us to be and do. Jesus told a story about three workers who were given different amounts of money by their employer before he left on a long trip. They didn't get instructions on what to do with the money, but two of the workers instinctively knew to get to work multiplying what they had been given. The other worker was too fearful, too risk-averse and chose not to maximize what she received. Maybe she was afraid of what people would think about her stepping outside of the box to do the thing God placed in her heart. Perhaps she thought it would be enough for her employer to focus on helping her husband be the best at what he was called to do.

But when the master came back to review what they had been doing, she quickly found out that she was wrong. She wasn't able to explain away her fear or hide behind her husband to justify why she didn't do all that she could with the investment that was made in her. What has God invested in you? Godly women know that all of us are accountable for what God gave us and will answer to Jesus for our fruitfulness or lack thereof.

A Godly woman is hospitable.

When my mother and aunt were children, my grandmother was known to be an amazing, from scratch everyday cook. She would make her own preserves, bake her own bread, and there was always a homemade dessert to enjoy every night. She was famous for her delicious culinary creations. What was even more remarkable, in my opinion, was the attitude of my mother's friends whenever they came over to my grandparents' house. Day after day, they would play outside, laughing and talking like kids, and then walk into my grandparents' home like they lived there to open up the refrigerator and see what they could eat that day. Oh, they would greet my grandmother first, and then proceed to help themselves to whatever food she had prepared. There was never a question of whether or not they were welcome to enjoy. They were much too accustomed to my grandmother's hospitality. They knew she would never let them be hungry while she was around with food to share.

A simple, working definition for hospitality is showing love or kindness to guests. Genuine hospitality is an extension of God's love toward humanity expressed through a personal, voluntary extension of the resources of your house and your heart toward others. It is much more than being able and willing to feed someone at your home or show them to a spare bedroom for a couple of nights. Hospitality is an attitude of the heart.

Hospitality is a value straight from God's core. The God that brought the children of Israel out of bondage in Egypt commanded them to treat strangers or immigrants as they would treat natives for the sake of God's name (Leviticus 19:33-34; Ezekiel 20:9).

Jesus explains that welcoming strangers is something he takes personally as if you had welcomed him (Matthew 25:36-40). The greatest act of hospitality any of us have experienced is Jesus coming to earth to live as an anointed human being and die to redeem us back into the family of God. There's no way that Godly women, or men for that matter, can neglect hospitality in our daily lives.

Not only is generosity to strangers a value dear to God's heart, but it is also a doorway for a complete turnaround to take place in the life of the giver. The hospitality Rahab showed to the Israelite spies in the book of Joshua changed her life forever. Her willingness to take in the foreign strangers who had come to take over Canaan was her entry point into covenant with God, even though she wasn't an Israelite. It didn't matter that she was a well-known prostitute because her decision saved the lives of her family members and catapulted her into the lineage of Jesus Christ. In fact, the spread of early Christianity throughout the Roman Empire was partly due to the "hospitality strategy" of meeting at each other's homes for meals to share the gospel and the generosity shown in meeting the financial needs of those who needed support. Imagine how fast news of their kindness must have spread during the first century, a time when there was no such thing as a social safety net like government welfare. Hospitality is a marker of God's preeminence in your life as a godly woman.

A Godly woman is strong.

God created women to have power and authority. Think back on our discussion on *ezer*, the word God used to describe women. Every time that word is used in the Bible, the surrounding context gives the impression that an *ezer* is strong, capable and ready for battle. Back in Genesis 3, God prophesied that it would be the seed of the woman that would crush the serpent's head. Ever since then, the enemy has been working to confuse and obstruct humanity from reaching our full potential in God. The enemy's strategy has been to use pride to put a wedge between us, using haughty, domineering attitudes in men and pop culture to reinforce a weak, frivolous, man-crazy image of women in the media. Strong women have strong voices for those who are vulnerable and oppressed. It's hard to speak up for someone else if you don't see yourself as able to carry the weight. If the enemy can get us to lower our expectations, then he can corrupt our self-esteem and diminish the way women are seen all over the world.

Sheerah, an architect from the tribe of Joseph, is an excellent example of a strong woman. Can you imagine being a city builder during a time when women couldn't even ask for a divorce? Sheerah built three cities that still have remains to this day (1 Chronicles 7:24). Two of those cities are scenes of some of the most amazing battles in the Bible, including when Joshua asked God to make the sun stand still so that his army could conquer their enemy. It must have taken strength, determination and some guts for a woman to insist on building cities instead of staying home or tending to flocks like most women did in her time. Strong women are not afraid to stand out or to speak up for what is right. In 2 Kings, Huldah the prophet did not hesitate to tell King Josiah what the

Lord had said about the nation of Israel, even though it wasn't probably what he wanted to hear. She was willing to tell the truth, even if it caused her to fall out of favor with the king, because she followed God's lead. Real strength does not always require brute force or physical intimidation, but it does require courage and good character.

Lipstick Leaders

Women in leadership is a touchy topic for many church folks. There is a great divide in church culture between those who believe that women should be seen as leaders and those who think that God intended for men to occupy most, if not all, leadership positions. Different people brought up in different traditions will interpret the Scriptures to agree with one perspective or another. But, as we have come to know, purpose is always going to be defined by the Creator. When we approach this topic from that perspective, we are sure to eliminate the tendency to keep the status quo when it is in disagreement with God's perspective. God always has the last word when it comes to why we are who we are. We know that women and men are jointly created in the image and likeness of God. We also know that every woman is an ezer, a sustaining help to overthrow an adversary. Let's put these two concepts together in a helpful identity equation:

Identity Equation:

Image and likeness of God (with men)

+

Help that overthrows an adversary (*ezer*)

____

The God-kind of help

God is the help that we cannot see. And women are the God-kind of help that can be seen. Men and women, partnered in presenting the full image and likeness of God, are empowered with the same authority and influence necessary to carry out our joint purpose. When God spoke humans into existence, all of the power required was immediately invested in us to stand up in our God-given identities and execute our God-ordained assignments. There's simply no other way we could make good on God's word if this were not the case. The image and likeness of God is our point of reference for identity and authority. That means we should first look at God to learn more about our Creator and then allow the Holy Spirit to reveal in us what measure of God's qualities live within us. Even though we all originate from the same source, we are all unique expressions of God's capacity, creativity, and character. The differences that we recognize in each other provide color and context for our life-long journey walking and talking with God. We have the amazing privilege of representing all of the beautiful qualities our God possesses to the rest of creation. In our unique ways and according to our individual purposes, we get to look and act like God. When we believe and behave in ways that are in alignment with this reality, we live fully submitted lives that are dedicated to embodying all that God had in mind for us and creation from the very beginning of human existence.

Unfortunately, we have not always stuck to God's plan. We have authority and influence within the scope of our unique, divine responsibilities that have been predetermined by God. When we overstep our boundaries, we inhibit the progress of others alongside us who need to take more accountability for how they show up in the world. When we fail to meet our potential, we unduly shift more burden and workload to others and simultaneously rob them of experiencing what God stored inside of us. Think of life on earth as a massive, complex group project for human beings. Have you ever been part of a group project for work or school? I bet you've had at least one memorable experience working with a group that just couldn't get it together. Maybe one of your teammates was a ball hog—always talking, always taking on too much responsibility, often assuming that his or her way is the best course of action. Or maybe you had a teammate that never seemed to get their work done, waited around hoping no one would notice their lackluster or non-existent contribution, and always had an excuse about why they couldn't keep up their end of the group assignment. Having to work with both overcompensaters and lazy folks is usually not a great experience for anyone. Why can't everybody just carry their own weight? But this is precisely the position God is often in when leading us into destiny. God told Jeremiah that he formed, knew and ordained him before he had even been conceived in his mother's womb (Jeremiah 1:5). I believe the same is true for all of us. God knew exactly what it would take to solve some of the world's most perplexing problems and responded to those challenges by creating us to be unique solutions, divinely positioned to enforce Jesus' victory over all the work of the enemy.

Every time one of us opts out of playing our position, we cause unnecessary interference in God's plan. The area of women in leadership, I believe, is one of the most attacked areas by the enemy. For millennia, various cultures have restricted or forbidden women to lead in the home, at work, and in ministerial office. Sadly, Christianity is no stranger to this ungodly tradition. Despite the many examples of bold, courageous women in the Bible, many of our churches and women's ministries have been satisfied with relegating women to leading prayer and children's ministries, and offered little to no thought leadership in alleviating the social, political and economic ills that women all over the world face daily. Many of us still believe that men are natural-born, God-ordained leaders in the home, at work and in religious life, simply by right of gender. The tradition of male headship has been supported by a creative theology that is not in alignment with the heart or word of God. You'll never find the scripture in the Bible in which God gives men the divine right to lead, installs men as head of household, or establishes men as the foundation of the family. Yet these are commonly accepted misconceptions based on incorrect Biblical interpretations and cultural biases that are designed to usurp the authority and influence not only of women but humanity as a whole.

If women are not fully empowered to exert our God-given influence and authority alongside men, then humanity is handicapped and unable to fully execute our divine responsibilities. Throughout the Bible, the Church, like all other nations, is identified as feminine. Is it a coincidence that the Church is called the bride of Christ? Is it a coincidence that the plight of women in the world seems to parallel the plight of the modern

Church in the world —unduly lacking power, authority and influence? What would happen if the Church was seen as second-in-command and incapable or unfit to lead? God forbid. In fact, many preachers have taught that the Church is the light of the world and the salt of the earth (Matthew 5:13-16). And it's true! As the body of Christ, we have a duty and responsibility to do the work that Jesus left for us until He returns. It's the Church's role to be a positive spiritual and moral influence on the world. And Jesus has given us his example and his inheritance to accomplish that very task. But if we are determined to restrict and confine leadership responsibilities to one gender, how effective can we really be? Instead of fully utilizing all of our resources, we have insisted on deliberately trying to run a race with only one of our arms and one of our legs. If we have no problem preaching that the Church should be helping to solve the world's problems, then we should have no problem releasing all women to fully embody the mission of the Church in every aspect of life.

And so, the first step to godly women leading well is

to believe. We have to first believe that we are called to lead. Believing takes courage— it's not always fun to stand out for believing something different than what's popular. I don't think anyone wants to be accused of stirring the pot or being a Jezebel or any of the other unkind accusations casually hurled at people who do not conform to popular opinion within our faith communities. You may not have the courage to say it out loud at first, but the more time you spend with God being affirmed in your real identity, the more Holy Spirit-inspired boldness will insulate you from anyone's rude comments, micro-aggressions and petty arguments. The faith you need to believe in the total equality of men and women may start as a grain of mustard seed, but as the roots of God's love grow deeper in your heart, you will find your confidence and your conviction grow stronger by the day.

Believing that women should lead is not carte blanche to take over every committee, fight to get your way, hog every microphone or demand obedience from everyone because the 'good 'ol days' of women being subservient to men are over. Freeing women to lead should not arrest men and put them into bondage. It doesn't mean that you will never submit to male authority figures again and it doesn't automatically place a woman in charge of everything. The only commandment godly women (and men) are bound to is love. Our intentions, conduct, and influence should always reflect our commitment to love others as Jesus loves us. An obnoxious, domineering attitude from a man or a woman has no place in the kingdom of God. Men and women who lead can avoid the pitfalls of ego-centric leadership by emulating Jesus and studying many of the women in the Bible who exhibited exceptional leadership qualities.

Let's look at Deborah from the book of Judges. Deborah was a judge in Israel for forty years and also served as a prophet. She was a leader that juggled judging matters for the people and leading the army into battle. She encouraged Israel's army captain, Barak, to do what God told him to do. She prophesied fearlessly about how the battle against Israel's enemies would end before they had even started to fight. She foretold that a woman would get the credit for defeating Israel's enemy. Some have misinterpreted that prophecy and believed that she was implying that Barak was afraid and would be embarrassed by a woman defeating an enemy he was too scared to face. But Deborah just said what the spirit of God had revealed to her—nothing more, nothing less. Barak refused to go into battle without her, so he evidently considered her to be an invaluable asset to him and their war campaign. She wasn't afraid to share credit with others and encourage their capabilities, as evidenced by her partnership with Barak and their celebratory song about the woman who defeated the general of the opposing army. Deborah judged rightly and bore good fruit while she was in her position. After the battle, Israel enjoyed a long period of peace under her leadership. She must have served well to have such an excellent track record.

Society often tells women that it's impossible to "have it all"—to lead an accomplished life and enjoy a wonderful marriage. But the Bible tells us that Deborah was married while she was leading and protecting

Israel. When a woman is called to lead, God will ensure that every relationship ordained for her life will be supportive of her purpose. Deborah is an incredible example of leading well under pressure and championing others. Deborah is not the only woman from the book of Judges who stands out. It is Jael, a "woman of the tent," who killed Sisera, the army general of Israel's enemy. Jael did not have to be a trained warrior, a princess, a judge or a prophet to help God's people. In fact, you could say Jael was a housewife. She didn't need to have a fancy title or job to be in the perfect position when Sisera came to her looking for help. She only needed the courage to seize the opportunity and the skills she already had from setting up her family's tents to get the job done. She did not hesitate to outwit and outmaneuver the skilled warrior standing before her. She used wisdom she and accomplished what no one else could. God will always prepare you before God positions you. After she lulled him to sleep, she picked up the tent peg that she had picked up so many times before and drove it straight through Sisera's temple. When she was sure he was dead, she ran out to tell Barak what she did. She did not downplay her role or act bashfully about her conquest. What a woman! There are times when women will downplay their accomplishments to avoid appearing arrogant or making others feel inadequate or threatened. I hope what Deborah and Barak sang about Jael in Judges 5 encourages you:

> "Most blessed among women is Jael,
> The wife of Heber the Kenite;
> Blessed is she among women in tents. He asked for water, she gave milk;
> She brought out cream in a lordly bowl.
> She stretched her hand to the tent peg,
> Her right hand to the workmen's hammer;
> She pounded Sisera, she pierced his head,
> She split and struck through his temple.
> At her feet he sank, he fell, he lay still; At her feet, he sank he fell; Where he sank, he fell dead."

Maybe you have been taught that it's not a woman's place to do what Jael did. Her husband should have stepped up and taken care of this threat to Israel.

Wasn't he the protector and the priest of his home? Isn't it just the man's job to handle things like that? The only problem with that is that you can not find a single scripture in the Bible that gives men the responsibility of being the priest and the official protector of the home or in any other capacity, for that matter. Tradition has dictated certain roles for men and women in the home and society, but God's Word trumps tradition every time. Godly women lead well because we believe. We believe in ourselves and we believe in causes that are bigger than our desires and need for comfort. We believe even when the odds are stacked against us. We believe even when we don't feel qualified to get the job done or worthy enough to be considered. God tends to qualify you in ways that you don't expect. The next time you're facing an obstacle or opportunity, ask yourself the following questions:

• What am I doing with the opportunity that God has given me?
• How am I moving the ball forward?

• Am I living up to the potential that God has placed on the inside of me?

Sometimes it's hard to do what you know needs to be done because you are afraid. Fear does a great job of making people feel small and powerless. It's a common misconception that great leaders do not feel fear. Nothing could be farther from the truth. Leaders feel the fear— but they don't allow the fear to boss them around. This is especially true of those who feel led to stand up for others like Esther did. I believe that the fasting and prayer Esther did before she saw the king gave her an extra dose of boldness. When she went before him and he asked her what she wanted, she did not hesitate to be clear in telling him exactly what she desired. There was nothing passive or timid about her approach. Great leaders always have a clear target in mind.

For many years, women have been encouraged to be soft-spoken, quiet or less direct when speaking or asking for something. If you strayed from that, there was a good chance that you would be labeled as "bossy" or some other unpleasant name. Many women's ministries and pulpit sermons have reinforced this idea, but the Bible is full of straightforward, assertive women. I believe that it has been the plan of the enemy all along to weaken the effectiveness and leadership ability of humanity by deceiving women into believing that we are not smart enough, emotionally stable enough, or just not suited for taking on leadership roles and speaking up for ourselves and others. We have been conditioned to believe that being quiet, soft-spoken and "going with the flow" (even if "the flow" is wrong) is more feminine than being direct, assertive, strong negotiators. But if Esther had lived up to that false feminine ideal, what would have happened to her people? If Jael had done that, what would have been the result? There is a famous quote that says "The only thing necessary for the triumph of evil is for good men to do nothing." Well, the same is true for women. When good women do nothing, we give permission for evil to have its way.

Our Proverbs 31 woman is called a woman of valor or might. This exemplary woman seems to have it all—

she's an entrepreneur, an excellent household manager, her husband and kids are happy, and she has an excellent reputation. She's described as a hard worker, dutiful and strong. She seems to be involved in a few businesses and skilled in each one of them. She's organized and plans ahead for herself and her family. All of these are great leadership traits, but there are two qualities that make her stand out: confidence and delegation. The Proverbs 31 woman has confidence in the value she provides to others.

> She perceives that her merchandise is profitable. Her lamp does not go out at night. Proverbs 31:18

What you have to give is profitable for you and others. So many women believe that what they think, say, feel and do has little to no impact on the world. When you downplay your value and worth, it sends a message to others to do the same. If you don't perceive what you have to offer as good, how will anybody else be able to receive from you? Being made in God's image makes you intrinsically valuable, even if you have a rough past and have made bad decisions. God's love for you can heal any broken self-image and restore your confidence. Once your self-esteem is intact, your sense of expectation that something good will come out of what you do will grow over time. That's why her candle didn't go out at night—she was so confident in what she had to give, that she stayed up working and preparing to give her very best. She knew that she was going to bless somebody, solve a problem, help someone and she wanted to be ready. Purpose always stokes the fire of expectation. She had good expectations and worked to ensure her expectations were met.

The Proverbs 31 woman's other "superpower" was delegating responsibility to others. Proverbs 31:15 details that she provided portions for her servants. While many may skim over this verse, it's worth taking a moment to consider that this woman, who is quite productive, was not trying to accomplish everything by herself. When is the last time you asked for help? The Proverbs 31 woman positioned herself to operate at her highest level by delegating to others. She had help!

Some women are taught to do everything themselves, even when it's not the best use of their time or energy. Some women even take on responsibilities that others are more than capable of handling, even if it doesn't get done exactly the way you would do it. The best leaders, at home and in the workforce, know that everybody needs help from time to time. Now you may or may not be in a position to hire someone to clean your home, cook your food or be a personal assistant, but there are other ways that people can help. Look around and ask yourself, "Do I have to do this or do I have another option?" Do yourself a favor and don't rule out giving up some of the control over how things get done to other people. Give someone else a chance to learn, grow and shine in an area that doesn't require your full attention. Delegating to others will help you to serve as the highest and best version of yourself.

All of these attributes help us to maximize our God-given capacity for leadership. For many of us, the first and hardest step toward leadership will be making the decision not to be a bystander. Every leader has a learning curve, but we still have to get in the game.

Romans 8:19 tells us that all of creation is waiting for the revealing of God's real children. As sons and daughters of God, we have a responsibility to fulfill God's expectation that we would be faithful and just stewards over the rest of creation. Equality is inclusive of duty and privilege. The world is counting on us to lead together and lead well.

Let's Stay Together

There is a profound revelation in God's statement that humankind should not be alone or "all one." At first glance, however, it doesn't really make sense. How could a perfect human, walking and talking with God all day, be in need of anything or anyone? So often, we think that we're perfectly fine as long as we can manage our responsibilities without too much trouble. It is a blessing to have everything you need and be fully capable of handling what life throws in your direction. But I believe God saw an opportunity to give mankind an experience not yet enjoyed—partnership. Without another human being to walk, talk and rule within the garden, our first human ancestor would have missed out on the benefits of learning to trust, learn from, care for and teach another person. God knew this and created women to demonstrate the value of partnership and companionship. We already know from studying the word *ezer* that God envisioned men and women to work together as one with a common purpose, not work against each other. In God's eyes, anything God has brought together cannot be split apart (Mark 10:8). Unfortunately, our ancestors chose to trade their God-given identities for ones of their own making by listening to the serpent in the garden. As soon as God found them after they ate the fruit, they started playing the blame game instead of taking responsibility for their bad choices. Since then, we have struggled to live harmoniously with each other in a way that honors God's intentions.

Historically, women have been considered property, second-class citizens, and unfit for positions of authority or leadership in every sphere of society. For example, it has only been within the last hundred years that women in the United States of America have enjoyed the privilege of voting in elections or opening a bank account without legal permission from a husband or father. Men all over the world have been taught that genuine masculinity is synonymous with dominance, headship and disproportionate authority and responsibility in the home, workplace, and society at large. While many strides have been made to right-size our skewed perceptions, we still have some ways to go in walking in the liberty that God intended.

> Where the spirit of the Lord is, there is liberty.
> 2 Corinthians 3:17

If we are to live according to the standard established in the Word of God, then we must commit to a framework that respects freedom. We must commit to a lifestyle that embraces the justice and righteousness of God for every human being. When our Adam ancestors lost their intimate relationship with God, they also lost a true understanding of their identities that drastically altered their relationship with each other. They had to leave their home and live a hard life because they did not listen to and believe God. Evil and wickedness became the standard way of life and death started the long process of decay and destruction in the earth. But God always had a plan to put the family back together, and that plan unfolded through many generations. God chose certain people to play critical roles in this plan—some were businessmen, some were royalty, some were shepherds, some were foreigners, some were special messengers, and many others participated in God's plan. Their lives and destinies span thousands of years, wars, periods of exile, bloodshed, times of peace and times of great miracles. Ultimately, all of these events point to the arrival of God's chosen son, Jesus the Christ. Conceived by God's spirit and born of a virgin woman, Jesus is the one God chose to unite the family of God and destroy every evil work.

Jesus lived and died to reunite all human beings with God, our Creator. We were unable to live up to God's standard of uprightness and were heading down a path of death and destruction for all. But God loved us so much that Jesus was sent to us to live among us and teach us about God in a way that had not been done before him. He did all of this while upholding God's standard of righteousness. When the right time came, Jesus died to satisfy the debt accrued by our failures and shortcomings—past, present and future. Since justice had been satisfied, God welcomed us back into the family and our rightful place as rulers and caretakers of the earth. When Jesus came back to life, he took on his responsibility as the supreme ruler of all rulers. He gave us power and authority to rule in life and to overcome all of the evil that has overtaken the world. He then sent us his Holy Spirit to guide us in relating to God and each other the way God always intended. This specific assignment of the Holy Spirit is called justice.

We tend to think of justice as retribution for wrong or taking legal action to punish someone. In ancient Hebrew culture, the concept of justice was centered around the pursuit and preservation of right relationships. In fact, justice and righteousness are often discussed together in the Hebrew Bible. You can't have justice without righteousness, because righteousness is what tells us what is right and wrong in any given situation. According to Proverbs 11:1, God detests "a false balance" and is pleased with a "just weight." While the verse's immediate reference is to business dealings, the principle of God's love for justice applies to every aspect of our human relationships. Injustice is vile and disgusting in the eyes of God. Once Jesus died to restore us, we were made perpetually righteous in God's eyes. There is nothing we did to earn this status; we simply inherit it due to what Jesus accomplished. While that is an amazing benefit for us as individuals, there are still "false balances" that persist in our relationships with each other. We are tasked with aligning our perceptions of and actions toward others in a way that mirrors the God-given righteousness we personally experience as a result of the free gift Jesus gave.

Righteousness is a perpetual state of right or pleasing relationships according to God's character. Our righteous identity impacts every area of our lives. Throughout our lives, each of us will engage in both vertical and horizontal relationships. Our vertical relationships start with how we relate to God and include our relationships with authority figures, the government, employers, elders, and children (if you are a parent). Vertical relationships are identified by the additional honor, or increased responsibility others have in relation to us or that we have with regard to others. For example, the relationship between a parent and a child is a vertical relationship. The relationship between a government and its citizens is also a vertical relationship. Horizontal relationships are identified by a shared investment of responsibility on a peer-to-peer basis. Friendships, extended family, neighbors, coworkers, fellow volunteers, and strangers are all examples of horizontal relationships. Righteousness seeks to maintain harmony in both our vertical and horizontal relationships by honoring people appropriately and actively seeking out opportunities to "do justice" to those in need. The Bible mentions justice and righteousness more often than love, heaven, hell, and wealth. There are over 300 scriptures that mention justice and righteousness, and many of the messengers God sent to us before Jesus came spoke about the need for justice to be done.

"How long will you judge unjustly and show partiality to the wicked? Selah. Give justice to the weak and fatherless; maintain the right of the afflicted and destitute. Rescue the weak and the needy; Deliver them from the hand of the wicked."

Psalm 82: 2-4

Over and over, God speaks to how vital justice is within every sphere of society. God expects us to be champions of justice in every capacity whether it is being kind to neighbors or standing up for people who cannot stand up for themselves. Justice is so important to God that it is the foundation of God's authority, according to Psalm 89:14.

Restoring right relationships between men and women is not a civil rights issue. It is not limited to any one government or the culture of one nation. The equality of men and women is a matter of God's idea of justice and righteousness. One area in which justice and righteousness for men and women must be pursued is in the structure of the family. God's original plan for the human family was for men and women to partner together in ruling over and taking care of the earth. Unfortunately, one of the negative consequences of our Adam ancestors' unbelief was the birth of the battle of the sexes. We see the immediate impact of this in the naming of the woman.

Before they listened to the snake, they were both known as Adam. After God explained the outcomes of their actions, however, the man ends up in a dominant position over the woman. It's important to realize that this shift takes place as a result of their poor decisions, and God never endorses this new arrangement. Right after God finishes explaining the consequences of their actions, the man names the woman Eve and the separation between them is memorialized. Men and women, from that point on, co-existed in this unholy system of hierarchy.

Many have been taught that male headship in the home is the natural order of the family. In fact, some have even been taught that the male position of leadership in the family makes men the foundation of society-at large. Make no mistake—the belief that men are the foundation of society or that husbands are the heads of households is a direct result of prideful traditions. It is pride that exalts the importance, power or influence of one person over another to their detriment. It is pride that engenders the arrogance undergirding the idea of male superiority and female inferiority. It is pride that replaces God's stated intention for men and women to rule together as partners with an inferior lifestyle that requires the subjugation of women to men. Prideful men and women have created and supported traditions within every sphere of society that perceives women to be less than men.

Since the family is the basic building block of society, the lessons taught and reinforced about masculine and feminine identity inevitably seep outside of the privacy of our homes into every public arena. In our modern times, we like to think of ourselves as able to compartmentalize our beliefs and separate our private thoughts from our public actions. But we are not designed to live that way. The Bible tells us in Luke

8:17 that whatever is hidden will eventually be disclosed. As long as we hold onto any shred of a perception that men and women are not equal, at home and everywhere else, we will continue to see sexism and patriarchy cheat us out of our human potential. Pride is a thief that ultimately aims to steal God's glory and it will exploit character weaknesses, ignorance and low self-esteem to achieve its end.

Preachers and teachers have used various statements from the apostle Paul's letters to the churches in Corinth and Ephesus to support the idea of male headship in the home. Much of this belief centers on the way the letters have been translated from the original languages into English and our modern understanding of certain words. Since the Bible was transcribed thousands of years ago and translated several centuries ago, it's essential that we read for context and content. It would be a mistake to impose our modern sensibilities on ancient culture and language.

The metaphorical use of 'head' in 1 Corinthians 11 is

commonly read as a hierarchical order of human beings and God. But the scripture is not conveying positional order or authority. It is part of a conversation about worship practices in the Corinthian congregations.

> But I want you to understand that the head of every man is Christ, the head of a wife is her husband, and the head of Christ is God. 1 Corinthians 11:3

If Paul's intention was to establish a rank order, why not start with God and end with mankind? If he had begun his statement with God as Christ's head and Christ as man's head, then that would have been consistent with establishing a hierarchy. But that is not what Paul wrote. Further, if Paul's actual statement was intended to show rank, then he would be positioning Jesus under God. But Jesus himself said that he and God are equal in John 15:17-18, so that would have been quite a contradiction.

Kephale is the Ancient Greek word that is translated as head in English. It has a few meanings, just like the English word. Its primary meaning, however, is the literal head of a person or an animal. At times, it can connote the beginning or source of something, like the head of a river. The Hebrew equivalent of *kephale* is the word *rosh*, which forms a familiar phrase from Genesis, *Bresheet*, or 'In the Beginning.' In order for us to understand what the author means to say, we have to pay attention to the context of the statement. Each time Paul mentions the word 'head' or *kephale*, he is using a metaphor relating Jesus' relationship with His followers to the anatomy of a human body. In Paul's mind, Jesus is the 'head' and we are the 'body of Christ.' *Somatos* is the Greek word that means the body of a human or an animal. In Ancient Near East cultures, the head was not considered the center of decision-making for a person. This is different from our modern times in which we devote a lot of attention to our brain power. Instead, the head was considered the most prominent or recognizable portion of the body. Also, the head is the first body part to emerge from the womb during childbirth. Think of this when you read

Colossians 1:18 or 2:19 in which Paul conveys that Jesus is the firstborn of the brethren and the "head" to which the "body of Christ" must remain connected. Think of your own body: do people recognize you by your shoulders or your kneecaps? Probably not. It is most likely that people recognize you by face. Do you think of your head as separate from your other body parts? Of course not! Your head and your body are one—united in identity, efficacy, and purpose. People don't call your head by your first name and your elbows by some other name. When someone calls you by name, they are calling your entire person— spirit and body. This is the point that Paul is trying to make whenever he mentions the head and the body in relation to Christ and believers—we are united with Jesus always. We are one with Him. We are recognized as Christ-partakers when we"look" like him. The human body is one and singular, with no part outranking the other. While the brain sends the signals that tell each member how to respond, the body is what moves and makes an impact on whatever is within its range of motion. Neither is of much use without the other. A body and its head have a mutual dependence and need for each other.

Many would say that Jesus is the leader of the Church or the 'body of Christ.' Indeed, Jesus should be showed honor in all things. Jesus led us in being born of the spirit first and being born from the dead first (Matthew 1:18; Colossians 1:18). We look to Jesus as the pattern for our new identity, as a new human species with authority and power and values from the kingdom of God (2 Corinthians 5:17; Ephesians 1:19-23). The idea, however, that Jesus is leading or controlling our every decision is false. Indeed, the Holy Spirit guides us into all truth and tells us what is right and wrong (John 16:8,13). Ultimately, we still retain the power of agreement. We decide when we will agree with what is right and when we will not. Have you ever decided to do something that you knew wasn't right in God's eyes? Jesus was not leading you into making that decision. He was not acting as your "head" in the sense of commanding you in what to do. Instead, he was with you while you were in the wrong and helped you get back on the right side of things.

The same way your head doesn't float off your shoulders when your body turns in the wrong direction is the same way that Jesus will not abandon you when you behave wrongly, whether it was intentional or unintentional.

Paul was a native Greek speaker writing to other native Greek speakers. He wrote to all of the churches in the common Greek dialect to ensure they could understand him well. When Paul or other New Testament writers are communicating that someone is a leader over others, they use the Greek word *archon*. This word means ruler, chief or prince. Mark 10:42 is a good example of how it was typically used. Notice that it was never used when describing the relationship between men and women or the relationship between Jesus and the Church. If Paul intended for his audience to think along those lines concerning male-female or husband-wife relationships, then it would have been much simpler to use *archon* instead of *kephale* to imply there should be a chain of command in their personal relationships.

In Ephesians, Paul is quoted as saying that wives should be subject to their husbands. Submission can be a controversial topic in the church. Let's take a closer look at the translated original text:

> Submitting yourselves to one another in reverence to Christ. Wives, ~~submit~~ to your own husbands, as to the Lord. For the husband is the head of the wife even as Christ is the head of the church, his body, and is himself its Saviour. Now as the church submits to Christ, so also wives should ~~submit~~ in everything to their husbands.
> Ephesians 5:21-24 (emphasis added)

The Greek words *hupo* and *tassó* form a compound word that is translated into English as 'submission' or 'be subject under.' We see this word used when disciples cast out demonic spirits in Jesus' name (Luke 10:20). *Hupo* is a word that often means 'by, through, or under.' *Tassó* is a word that means 'arranged or in specific order.' One way to interpret *hupotasso* is 'by arrangement" or "under a specific order." Upon reviewing this word *hupotasso*, we see that there is an added dimension of meaning that has been lost in translation. In fact, some Greek dictionaries report that *hupotasso* is a Greek military term meaning to "arrange {troop divisions} in a military fashion under command of a leader[7]. First, notice that Paul tells the congregation to *hupotasso* each other. Since Paul's letters were read out loud to the entire group, comprised of men and women, we can safely conclude that Paul expected both men and women to *hupotasso*. Second, *hupotasso*, or submission, only appears twice in the original text. In English translations, wives are given specific instructions to *hupotasso*, but this was added by the translators. Adding the word puts emphasis on women or wives that Paul did not intend to be there. In context, Paul is again using the metaphor of human anatomy to persuade the congregation that man-woman or husband-wife relationships should align to the loving example of Christ and the Church. Earlier in Paul's letter to the Ephesians, he states that believers, as Christ's body, are seated with Jesus in heavenly places at God's right hand. Every principality, power, and authority is under his feet, so that would place them underneath us also. There is no suggestion of gender-based disparity in position or influence within the body of Christ. We occupy the same seat as Christ and are joined to him. In essence, the use of *hupotasso* suggests that the "troops" need to be lined up by the arrangement of the leader. We know from Genesis that the right leader for humankind is God. God is the one who determines what is good and what is right. We are to be led by God, just as our Adam ancestors initially were led in the garden of Eden. There was no spiritual or earthly rank between man and woman in the beginning, nor did they have an intermediary between them and God. God gave them one name (Genesis 5:2) and one assignment (Genesis 1:26). It was only in their unbelief and disobedience that they came out of oneness with each other, started blaming each other and men began to dominate women (Genesis 3). God's arrangement was for men and women to be peers, counterparts, and united in purpose to overthrow the adversary. Our made-up arrangement for men and women is inferior to what God originally designed. Deciding for ourselves what is good and right has born the tell-tale fruit of oppression, wrongful discrimination, and sexism. We have been taught that men or husbands should be the head of the household and some have even taught that men or husbands are the priests in the home. The problem is the Scriptures do not support this teaching. There is only one place in the Bible that states that men should be the head of the household, and it is not found where most preachers and teachers have told us to look:

> If it please the king, let a royal order go out from him, and let it be written among the laws of the Persians and the Medes so that it may not be repealed, that Vashti is never again to come before King Ahasuerus. And let the king give her royal position to another who is better than she. So when the decree made by the king is proclaimed throughout all his kingdom, for it is vast, all women will give honor to their husbands, high and low alike. This advice pleased the king and the princes, and the king did as Memucan proposed. He sent letters to

all the royal provinces, to every province in its own script and to every people in its own language, that **every man be master in his own household** and speak according to the language of his people.

Esther 1:19-22 ESV (emphasis added)

If you've ever read the book of Esther, then you know that the Persian king was married to Queen Vashti before he was married to Esther. When he commanded that Vashti be brought before him and she did not come, he and his counselors were angered and conspired together to punish her and send a message to the other women in the empire. They wanted to make sure that the women "knew their place," so they convinced the king to issue an irrevocable decree that every man is the master or leader in his household. This is the only scripture in the Bible that positions men in this way, and it is coming out of the mouth of a Persian king who did not worship God.

While God is never explicitly mentioned in the book of Esther, God's presence and providence was certainly felt throughout the text. Shortly after the decree goes out, a beautiful, Jewish refugee named Esther ends up becoming King Ahasuerus' wife and successfully averts an evil plot to kill all of the Jewish people in the kingdom. At the urging of her uncle Mordecai and with considerable bravery, she convinced the king to issue decrees in favor of her people staying alive and being empowered to retaliate against their enemies. When the king gives Mordecai his signet ring as a sign of authority, it is Esther that gives Mordecai a special position as a royal advisor.   When Mordecai encourages the Jews to commemorate this victory in an annual celebration called Purim, it is Esther's decree made in her own name that solidifies the plans and is published in every language and sent to all 127 provinces. Isn't it interesting that the only scripture that positions men over their households is found in a book named for a woman who literally issues the final word? God has quite the sense of humor.

It is time for men and women to be peers in every sphere of society, including in our homes. The leader we both should follow is God. God is more than qualified to be the head of every household, and it would be best for our homes to be arranged as God originally designed. We all have unique gifts, assignments, skills, and aptitudes that can qualify us for authority, rank or influence in any given area. But gender should not dictate how we assign leadership responsibility or privilege. God has made it perfectly clear that both men and women can lead in any setting.

Jesus Is Not a Feminist

In the beginning was the Word, and the Word
was with God, and the Word was God.
John 1:1

God's original design intended men and women to have equal and equitable dignity in every facet of life. This dignity and equality is rooted in humanity's origin in the image and likeness of God and cannot be achieved or replicated without God's direct involvement. We don't know how to be equal or free or human without God. None of those words meant anything until God defined them. Spiritual laws are always activated no matter what country, tradition, denomination, or time in human history we find ourselves. What was true in the beginning is still true now.

In the beginning, God created male and female human beings in the image and likeness of God and endowed both of us with the responsibility of managing the earth that God created. At no point was a special or additional assignment given to men to bear more responsibility than women. In fact, God said that it was not suitable for all of that responsibility to rest on one human's shoulders. It was only after the woman was introduced into humanity that God said creation was "very good." It was God's intention for both men and women to reflect the character of God and rule the earth. If we truly believe that we are equally and equitably made in God's image and likeness, then how can we believe in any human's inherent superiority over another human? It is our source that determines our value and our esteem, not our attributes.

Imagine looking God in the face and saying, "Hey, I think the left side of your face is your best side." I venture to guess that no one in his or her right mind would think or say such a thing, yet society insists on unjustly discriminating against human beings on the basis of sex and ethnicity. Quite literally, men and women are cut from the same "cloth." God's idea from the beginning is that we, as humans, are one image of God with two representations, man and woman. Two whole, complete representations of the same image of God. The oneness of humanity is reflected in the lack of individual names for humankind, as they were both referred to as Adam. In fact, there is no record in the Bible of God ever referring to the first woman as Eve. As far as God is concerned, we were, and still are, one.

We know the story of our Adam ancestors' fateful encounter with the serpent and their exile from the garden of Eden. When God explains the consequences of their actions, the woman ends up being in subjection to the man. Instead of enjoying an equal role in ruling the earth, the woman and all women after her were resigned to subservience and engaging in an endless power struggle with men.

Instead of serving as a strong *ezer* as God intended, women, as helpmeets, are often cast in a second-in-command role that defers to a man in all of society's power and cultural arenas. Thankfully, God has never forgotten about the daughters. Throughout the Bible's historical accounts, there are women whose bravery and influence foreshadow the re-emergence of God's daughters. Women like the daughters of Zelophehad, Sheerah, Jehosheba, Esther, Ruth, Jael, Deborah, Huldah and more that whisper of the true glory of being a Godly woman—strong, decisive, faithful, powerful, and bold. Ultimately, the catastrophic decision of our ancestors set a course of events in motion that would lead to our eventual redemption by the man Jesus Christ. Jesus' sole purpose was to bring the kingdom of God back to the earth and redeem the family of God back to our rightful relationships with God and each other. This redemption Jesus procured for all humanity liberated us from the deathly effect of sin and our warped relationships with God, self and others. Make no mistake—Jesus' justice mission accomplished the liberation of women from broken self-image and a skewed societal perception of a woman's worth. But none of this makes him a feminist.

There are well-meaning men and women of faith claiming to be Christian feminists because they rightly believe in gender equality. After all, the most basic definition of feminism is the belief in the political, economic and social equality of the sexes. At first glance, this definition appears harmless and does not seem problematic for people of faith. But everything is not as it seems.

> For a good tree does not bear bad fruit, nor does a bad tree bear good fruit. For every tree is known by its fruit. People do not gather figs from thorns, nor do they gather grapes from a bramble bush.
> Luke 6:43-44

The philosophy of feminism has nothing in common with the gospel of the Kingdom. It is a false solution presented by the same spiritual wickedness that created the problem of sexism in the first place. It was the serpent who deceived the woman into believing that she was not already like God by being made in God's image. The Bible records that the man was with her when she was talking to the serpent and said nothing tocorrect it or her. In fact, the man also became convinced that eating the fruit from the tree of knowledge of good and evil would make him more of something that he already embodied. Their complicit participation in their degradation set in motion the vicious psychological warfare that sexism wages in the minds of men and women today. Sexism desires to divide men and women through chronic insecurity, self-absorption and unchecked lust for power over another person. Remember that God's intention was for men and women to rule together, not compete with each other for authority and influence. The devil has been a divider from the beginning and the tactics remain the same. Feminism looks like an answer to the problems that misogyny and patriarchy have created in our culture, but it is cut from the same wicked cloth.

Any philosophy that seeks to elevate a person without connecting them back to God is bound to create idolatry. Feminism does not advocate for spiritual equality at all. The problem with measuring equality through political, economic or social means is that all of the standards are man-made and subject to change. Political, social and economic equality only address the symptoms of injustice between men and women. The root of inequality is always spiritual since the idea of equality is a spiritual concept from the kingdom of God. Man-made philosophies that try to use God's concepts without giving glory to God will not succeed. Humans are not only social or political beings—we are spirit. The deep insecurity we created by separating ourselves from God can only be healed by accepting the love of God shown through Jesus Christ's life, death and resurrection for the sake of our reunion with the Creator. We don't need to be feminists, because truly being a follower of Jesus is already inclusive of gender equality. As we study Jesus and follow him, our warped self--images as men and women will evolve and transform us into the mature offspring of God that we were always destined to become. Outwardly, the oppressive systems and cultural norms we have created to unfairly discriminate against each other by sex (or anything else) will be deconstructed. But what does this look like? It looks like equal pay for equal work. It looks like the death of rape culture. It looks like an end to laws and customs that exist purely to control the free movement and self-determination of women around the world. It looks like fewer women and children living at or below the poverty line. It looks like more women serving in fields where women are traditionally underrepresented. It looks like more women in boardrooms and in pulpits. It looks like the end of the cultural stranglehold of the porn and sex trafficking industries. It looks like men who act more like Jesus in private and in public. It looks like women who believe in themselves as much as Jesus believes in women. It looks like Jesus being lifted up and drawing more people to him. It looks like freedom.

Divide and conquer is the oldest trick the devil played on us. It will take aggressive repentance and forgiveness to reshape our minds, hearts, and world around the reality of equality. But it is worth it. As believers, we owe it to the world to actually lead on this issue and set a standard that makes them thirsty for a God who truly is not a respecter of persons.

> "Truly, truly, I say to you, the Son can do nothing of his own accord, but only what he sees the father doing. For whatever the Father does, the son does likewise." John 5:19-20

Jesus said that he only did what he saw God do. That means it is safe to assume that whatever Jesus did and said was condoned by God. So how does that factor into Jesus' interactions with women?

Jesus honored women as fully human and regarded them as daughters of God. He included women as illustrations in his parables. He used everyday images of women making bread, looking for coins, lighting lamps to paint various pictures of the kingdom of God and our interactions with it. He risked his reputation and broke tradition by speaking with the Samaritan woman at the well (John 4). According to Jewish tradition, men who lived during that time did not talk to women in public—not even their own wives! Jewish people also did not hang out with Samaritans, so Jesus was truly rocking the boat by merely having a conversation with this woman. Jesus revealed himself to her as the Messiah, and she believed him. She went and told the whole town all about him, and they believed her. With one conversation, Jesus had turned this unworthy, second-class citizen into the first evangelist! The disciples looked at her and wondered why he bothered talking to her, but Jesus looked at her and saw an opportunity to bring more people back into relationship with God. Her testimony opened a door for him to teach in Samaria and the people believed in Him. How many women are poised to be used by God in the same way but have been overlooked just because of gender and sexist ideas about "a woman's place"?

Jesus honored the faith of the Syrophoenician woman even though she wasn't one of the chosen people of Israel (Matthew 15:21-28). She pleaded with him to heal her daughter, and he tried to brush her off. Her remarkable belief that he would help her, irrespective of her asking at the wrong time or breaking any social customs, impressed Jesus so much that she is one of only two people Jesus said had great faith. Imagine being an outsider and a woman who shouldn't even be approaching a man in public. You work up the courage to ask for what you really want, and then Jesus refuses to help you and calls you a dog! But you respond with such faith, such boldness, and such utter conviction— fully believing that this man would set aside the rules just for you. And Jesus did exactly what she asked. She had irresistible faith.

The Gospels tell the story of some Pharisees picking a fight with Jesus about divorce (Mark 10:1-12). Not only did he point them back to God's real intention for marriage, but he also explained to his disciples that divorce could be initiated by men and women alike. Even though he explained that divorce is not God's desire for marriage, he still affirmed that women could initiate divorce at their discretion. Even in a less-than-ideal situation, Jesus showed that he thought of women as fully human, responsible moral agents who are capable of making decisions for themselves. Jesus personally demonstrated the equality that God always intended for women. His dealings with women were countercultural in His time, but they should be normal for our time. We owe it to him to fully exhaust every benefit and blessing his life has made available to us. It is for freedom that Christ has set us free (Galatians 5:1) and we should endeavor to be free indeed.

Moving Forward

It may seem like rebuilding society, brick by brick, would take hundreds, maybe even thousands of years to fully realize equality for men and women. After all, we certainly did not arrive at our present circumstances overnight. Our traditions, superstitions, and stereotypes over the course of millennia have rendered us desperately in need of God's life-giving breath to remind us who we really are again. We are in a season of grace for renewal and our redemption is hovering overhead, waiting for us to have the courage and presence of mind to reach up and grab it. The time for God's daughters to step into our rightful place is now. All of creation is waiting for the manifestation of the sons of God (Romans 8:19). The sonship Paul wrote about is a call to mature development. The whole earth is waiting for humanity, for the true sons and daughters of God, to be revealed and recognized as solutionists with answers for the world's toughest problems. God has given us the Holy Spirit, the mind of Christ, and our redeemed identity as God's offspring to equip and empower us to redeem communities and nations. There's a wealth of opportunity just ahead of us. And the only thing you need to do is believe and prepare for it. Belief comes before behavior. Belief is the key that unlocks our identities and empowers us to move forward. We cannot repeat the mistake that our ancestors made by second-guessing and presuming to know more about ourselves than God. No one knows you better than God knows you. As we take steps to live out equality in our everyday lives, it's probable that questions or conflicts will arise. We need to rely upon the counsel of the Holy Spirit to reinforce God's love and perfect design for us. God loves us enough to distinguish each one of us with a unique identity, purpose and calling that is ours alone—not dependent upon your gender, ethnicity, marital status, family history or educational background. Your status as a child of the King supersedes every category. Faith has a way of becoming contagious. When others see that you are committed to being the person God created you to be, then they will begin to have the confidence to do the same. We need not be concerned with others feeling threatened or insecure because doing things God's way guarantees us victory. Sometimes we underestimate how much time we need to spend learning to trust God in a new way before we take a big leap of faith. Make sure that you are meditating on God's Word about identity, praying and allowing the Holy Spirit to address any lingering issues that have arrested your development in the past. We need to spend time just soaking up the goodness and love of God because that is what shifts our belief system. Our faith in what God has said about us works by our acceptance of God's love (Galatians 5:6). That is what is going to ultimately change our behavior. No one can out-behave belief. So, we're going to have to spend quality time digesting God's promises and beholding

God's character, so that we can be quick to believe whatever God has said to us.

Release the debt.

Women have endured a lot of undue hardship over the years. Even though all women have not had the same life experiences, it has been universally more difficult being a woman than to be a man in society. It has taken many years to secure the current personal freedoms that some women in the world enjoy—voting privileges, inheritance rights, financial independence, and others. This move of God toward equality has been unfolding for some time, and it is understandable to experience heartache, pain, bitterness or resentment when realizing that women have been living beneath God's privileges for so long. But we are still bound to love God and love others as we love ourselves. As followers of Christ, love is the law of the land and love compels us to forgive as we have been forgiven. Forgiveness is often easier said than done, but God has given us the grace to release people of the debt they owe us just as God has freed us from our debt. We will have to forgive men and women who have oppressed, abused, and mistreated people in an attempt to limit their potential or diminish their capacity. We will have to forgive governments for being discriminatory and unjust. We're going to have to forgive them, but quite frankly, we're also going to have to forgive ourselves for believing the lies we were told about the worth of women. God has already forgiven us for thinking less of ourselves than we should.

The path forward is paved with forgiveness, and our emotions will have to play catch-up to our decision to release the debt. Each time you encounter an offense or a sexist barrier, remember that Jesus has given us the authority to tread upon any evil obstacle in our paths (Luke 10:19). We are walking the path of forgiveness from a position of victory that is not up for debate. Our job is to believe in the victory Jesus has won for us and walk it out no matter what we see because there is nothing that the enemy can do to alter what God has already decided. We will exercise our God-given dominion on this earth, men and women together, and that is God's final word. If you choose to hold onto unforgiveness, to play small, to shrink instead of rise up as the highest and best version of yourself, you deny yourself the privilege of mirroring the character of God. We are not made in our own image—we are designed to reflect our Creator. Forgiveness doesn't make you a doormat or a pushover, and it doesn't mean that you will always enjoy close relationships with people who are intent on being offensive. There will be times when you will be confronted with inequality at home, at work or elsewhere and it is your responsibility to seek counsel from the Holy Spirit to determine what should be done. There is nothing passive about choosing to see yourself as God sees you. When you believe in your God-given worth, inequality of any kind will likely trigger a response from you to act. Whatever the Holy Spirit advises you to do will be consistent with the love and values of the kingdom of God.

Show Me.

There are many women who do not have a history of positive relationships with men. As you step into your redeemed identity, you may wonder how you can relate to men differently than how you have done so in the past. One of the most powerful things you can do on this journey to equality is to pray:

Lord,

Show me how to be your daughter.

God will answer you and reveal the exact places in your heart that need more attention and care. First, it could be that the Holy Spirit will start working with you about feelings of rejection or abandonment and start to change your mind about how you see yourself in that regard. It could be that the Holy Spirit will look into your heart and say,

"Daughter,

You've developed a hard outer shell over the years. Now you won't let people in, and it's hard for you to connect with people. Well, I'm going to love you into a softer version of you. And it's not because you're a woman, it is because I want you to be able to receive love just as well as you can give it."

Vulnerability is a requirement for any man or woman that wants to receive love. You cannot grab something if your hand is tightly clenched into a fist. You have to be able to let go, relax and trust that God is your defense and your protection. God is a better bodyguard for you than you can be to yourself—so retire from being your own security! Ask God for discernment, put it to good use and trust that the Holy Spirit will never steer you wrong.

Ask like Achsah.

You will need an extra dose of boldness to move forward into equality. The story of Achsah in the Bible is an excellent example of how to ask God for what you really want. Her story appears in Joshua 15 and Judges 1, so it's doubly important to pay attention. Her father was the famous spy Caleb, who was a mighty man of God with incredible faith. When it was time for her to get married, he challenged any potential suitors to win her hand by successfully conquering a particular city. When Othniel rose to his challenge, Caleb gave Achsah away and gifted her with a parcel of land in the desert. One day Achsah went to her husband to get him to ask her father for a field. The next thing that happens is a little strange. Instead of Othniel going to see Caleb, we find Achsah riding on her donkey to ask Caleb for herself. Caleb sees her coming afar off and asks her what she wants. Without hesitation, Achsah acknowledges the desert land he already had given to her and boldly asks him for a blessing in the form of springs to water the land. And Caleb gave her not one, but two sets of springs to water the land.

Perhaps you feel as though God has given you some dry land. Maybe you feel as though you were born into difficult circumstances or stuck with baggage you wish you could offload. Have you ever thought to yourself, "Listen, God, you knew how hard it would be for us. Why in the world would you make me a woman?" If you happen to be a woman of color, you may have even said, "Why would you make me a black woman?,"or "Why would you make me a Latina?," or " Why would you make me an Asian woman?" It can feel like you've been dealt a bad hand of cards when society holds your ethnicity and your gender against you. And it can leave you wondering why God would purposely give you such tough territory as a "gift." Achsah may have thought the same way when her father gave her a patch of desert with no water for irrigating the land. But she did what we should do—she asked for what she wanted to steward what she had been given.

It's curious that we never learn what Othniel's response was to her when she asked him to make the request. Maybe he is the one who told her to ask for herself. Sometimes, women are encouraged to be timid about letting others know how they feel or what they want. Achsah shows us that closed mouths do not get fed. She was not in a position where she could depend on her husband to save her the trouble of seeming pushy or inappropriate. Perhaps it would have been easier for Othniel to do the asking so that she didn't risk coming across as ungrateful. But she wasn't in a position to ignore what she wanted for the sake of appearances. She wasn't in a position to pretend like what she had been given was enough for her. So she went to her father for herself. God has provided for your dry land, too. But you will have to ask for what you want and expect to get it. Achsah got more than what she asked for —the upper springs were good for irrigating the land to make it fruitful, and the lower springs would collect the overflow for storage. Asking made her wealthy beyond what she expected. What are you praying for?

God made you on purpose. The circumstances that you have been born into are no match for the power of your purpose and identity. There is only one of you and God has said that you are "...very good." You are enough for the life that God has called you to live. Don't waste your time despising your womanhood. It is a privilege to be a woman, indeed a daughter of God. God has given you good land and good resources for your land. All you need to do is ask like Achsah.

One of One.

God is not in the business of making carbon copies. Billions of people live on the earth, and each person is a completely unique expression of God's image and likeness that has never been seen before and will never be created again. God is perpetually doing a new thing and does not continually innovate just for us to waste time trying to be like someone else. That means that your spiritual and physical genetic blueprint is immensely valuable. You are one of a kind, and you don't belong in a box that was never designed to fit you. You don't have to like pink to be a real woman. You don't have to dress in lace, ruffles, and sequins. You don't have to cook blue-ribbon meals or wear your hair long to reach your full feminine potential. All you have to do is be the woman God made you to be, and that will be more than enough.

It will take discipline not to fall back into old habits or old ways of thinking about our identities as women. The patterns of inferiority woven into our culture's portrayal of women are deeply ingrained and will take some work to unravel. Commit yourself to keep God's pace in your journey to equality. Make sure that you are connected to a community of like-minded men and women who are committed to seeing human beings fulfill our full potential. We will move forward together in the light of God's grace. That's how we're going to secure the promised land. That's how we're going to do God's image justice and accurately represent who God is in this world.

The Cost of Comfort

Why not just be satisfied staying the same? After all, is anybody really comfortable with the idea of women genuinely being equal? There are lots of men who aren't comfortable with it and, quite frankly, there are a lot of women who are uncomfortable with the responsibility that comes with being equal and free. For some women, it would be too much of a culture shock to strip away the excuse of being "just a girl." It's too easy for some to say, "Hey, that's not my job anyway!" or "It's a man's world." In the church, we could continue to ignore what the Word of God really says and conveniently carry on with husbands being the foundation of the family as the head of household. Looking at all of the traditional couples, you can easily say, "If it ain't broke, why fix it?" It can seem as though they have picture-perfect lives, happy homes and successful marriages—all while following an identity pattern that is outside of what God intended. If success means you look good to the world, but not to God, then what is your definition of success based upon? When God created women, He had no intention of creating someone second best. He had no implicit or explicit intention of creating someone inferior. Think about it— how can you be an *ezer,* a help, to someone if you are always a "damsel in distress"? It's kind of hard to contribute if you don't bring much to the table.

Why would God call us to help if we were not equipped to embody the word? It just doesn't make any sense. We have to come to a place where we will not settle for anything less than what God said. Not because we're determined to have our own rights because this isn't about women's rights. And it's not about being upset or bitter, because you haven't forgiven someone for discriminating against you and treating you in a way that is beneath your real worth. It's not about being a victim or getting revenge. This is about love. Daughters, God loves us. Always has and always will. When God looks at us, God doesn't see someone who needs a male "covering" or someone that can't make it in life without a man's approval or sponsorship. God doesn't see someone who lacks the intellectual capacity or emotional stability to make high-quality decisions. God sees someone that looks and acts like a duplicate of kind— a game-changing, life-saving, make-it-happen human being that gets all of her power and grace from him. God sees so much of his own image in us, that the scriptures refer to God by the same word, *ezer*, that he used to define the essence of a woman. Take a minute and reflect upon the truth of that statement. There's nothing about women that's insufficient because God is not insufficient. There's nothing about women that is incapable because God is not incapable. There is nothing inherent in the makeup of a woman that makes her subordinate because God is not inherently subordinate.

Now, consider why we have allowed the image and identity of women to be twisted into perpetual subordination, insufficiency, and incapability. Consider how many women do the same work as men but are not equally compensated. Consider the toxic beliefs that have allowed pornography, global sex trafficking, and sexual harassment to persist within our culture. Consider the invisible ceilings that keep women from occupying high-ranking positions in various industries. Consider the still-raging debate within the Church about whether or not women should be allowed to preach, pastor or hold leadership roles within congregations. None of these present realities were in the heart and mind of God when creating us. And if you really love God, don't you want to see God's plans come to life? Don't you want God's wishes to be honored above anything else? Can we just love God enough to be ourselves? Can we stop forcing ourselves into playing roles that we were never meant to play?

What about Jesus? Jesus came to rescue us from some bad decisions that our ancestors made. Should we just neglect everything that Jesus won for us? Should we settle for being sort-of free, just enough to set everyone else at ease? Will we leave the wisdom, strength, riches, honor, glory, and power that Jesus died to receive and share with us as our joint inheritance (Revelation 5:12; Romans 8:17) on the table untouched because it's not our place to wield them? Will we refuse to sit on the throne we share with Jesus at God's right hand, because we are not man enough to do so?

No. We are enough. We are woman enough to fully apprehend all that God has destined for God's children. We are entirely responsible for what we do with the gifts God has given us. We do not get to abdicate the throne and be seated in God's presence at the same time. The time has come to choose in whom we believe. Traditions or God? Will we refuse to rule? Will we refuse to exert the authority and the judgment that Jesus came to this earth, lived a whole human life, and died to provide for us? God forbid.

We will not make a mockery of the blood of Christ by continuing to accept this unholy inferiority complex designed by the enemy to frustrate the plans of God. We will not dishonor his obedience and his love for us by living beneath our potential. We will not leave the work Jesus left for us undone. The time has come to love Jesus more than we love our own comfort. The time has come to honor Jesus more than we honor the opinions of others. When we fail to speak up for what is right, we conflate peace with quiet. Peace is not defined by silence, but by the forceful removal of chaos. How many lives hang in the balance of quiet complacency? How many destinies go unrealized in the name of going with the flow? How far does the culture have to fall before we are willing to use all of our weapons to fight against the lies the enemy has sown into our hearts and minds about our relationship with God and, by extension, our identities? As a body, we have been fighting this culture war with one hand tied behind our back for no reason. Sure, every hundred years or so a whisper of freedom comes and loosens the knot. But now God is calling us into absolute freedom. We must be free of restraints to overthrow our adversary successfully. We have to be free to help. Free to *ezer*.

Somehow we have bought into the lie that a husband and children make a woman complete, instead of purpose. Our relationships with others are vital and fulfilling, but the most important relationship in a woman's life is her relationship with God— and by extension, herself. The day is coming, sons and daughters. The day is coming when we will have to answer for what we believe and in whom we believe. We will have to answer for what we have done with what we have been given —all of the gifts and assignments God encoded within our DNA before we were ever born. We will answer for what we have brought to bear in this world and for what we have left dormant and undone. As followers of Christ, our judgment day is not based on how many sins we've committed. Jesus has already taken care of that. No, our judgment determines our reward. Jesus will decide whether what we have done or not done, what we have believed or not believed, is pleasing to him and reward us accordingly (Matthew 25).

It is our privilege to please Jesus in being who we are and through what we do. Being a feminist will not be what sets you apart. Treating your life's calling like a hobby will not set you apart. Raising amazing children, while rewarding and fulfilling in its own way, will not set you apart. Being the perfect wife to your husband will not set you apart. Climbing to the heights of your industry for the sake of the climb will not set you apart. None of us will be able to hide behind a label, a title, a last name, or a tradition. Only what we do for Christ will stand.

Yahweh Elohim has called you by your name, esteemed you worthy of honor and service, and separated you unto a unique calling that only you can fulfill. What you do with that calling is between you and God. Let the fear of the Lord inspire you to be the best human being you can be every day. Live your life as an answer, because you were created to be one. It's wisdom to be who God created you to be and healthy to do what God created you to do. It is up to us to have the courage to answer the call. It is up to us to take our position on the throne. The authority is already yours. The permission has already been granted. Daughters, you have already been crowned.

Notes & Additional Resources

1. "Definition Of IMAGE". Merriam-Webster.Com. https://www.merriam-webster.com/dictionary/image.

2. "Strong's Hebrew: 3335. יָצַר (Yatsar) – To Form, Fashion". Biblehub.Com. http://biblehub.com/153ebrew/3335.htm.

3. "Alone | Origin And Meaning Of Alone By Online Etymology Dictionary". Etymonline.Com. https://www.etymonline.com/word/alone.

4. "Shame | Definition Of Shame In English By Oxford Dictionaries". Oxford Dictionaries | English. https://en.oxforddictionaries.com/definition/shame.

5. Holy Bible: Kenneth Copeland Reference Edition. Reprint, Fort Worth, Texas: Kenneth Copeland Ministries, Inc., 1991.

6. "Chapter 2." Genesis: Translation and Commentary, by Robert Alter, Norton, 1997, p. 9.

7. "Hupotasso – New Testament Greek Lexicon – New American Standard". Bible Study Tools. https://www.biblestudytools.com/lexicons/greek/nas/hupotasso.html.

Additional resources:

- *In The Spirit We're Equal: The Spirit, the Bible & Women, A Revival Perspective* by Susan C. Hyatt
- *Fashioned To Reign: Empowering Women to Fulfill Their Divine Destiny* by Kris Vallotton
- *God's Word to Women* by Katherine C. Bushnell
- *Paul, Women and Church* by Eddie Hyatt
- *The Future War of the Church*, Chapter 9: Women Arising Now

Crowned Prayer

Lord, I believe that you love me. I am who you say that I am. I can do what you say that I can do. I resist all of the lies that tell me I am not enough because I am a woman. Help me to renew my mind and see myself the way you see me (James 4:7; Rom 8:26; Eph 4:22-24; Rom 12:2)

I take my rightful place on the throne with Jesus at your right hand. I lay hold of every part of my inheritance. I cut off every lie that the enemy has told me about womanhood. I reject all pride, insecurity, confusion and perversion of my God-given identity in Jesus' name. I do not tolerate bondage any longer. I accept that I am made in your image and likeness. I take after you and look like you. I have your DNA in my spiritual DNA (Eph 1-2:6; Gal 4; Phil 4:13; Gen 1:26).

Now I take up my authority and ask for your counsel and wisdom in how to use it. I expect to hear from you daily. Teach me about myself and tell me your plans for me. I loose freedom in my mind and in every area of my life (Luke 10:19; James 1:5; Jer 29:11; Gal 5:1)

Thank you for making me victorious!
(1 Cor 15:57)

In Jesus' name, Amen!

Love Power Prayer

This daily love declaration was born out of a personal epiphany I had about God's love for me and the essentialness of the love nature to being a true follower of Christ. As I adopted this prayer into my daily routine, I quickly saw a positive change in my emotional health and a dramatic improvement in all of my relationships. Love is the key to lasting change in any Christian's life and I encourage you to meditate on God's love and put it into action every day.
God bless you!

Father God, I thank you for empowering me with love; for of faith, hope, and love, love is the greatest of them all. Because of your holy example, I am patient with people & I am kind to others. I do not envy others. I do not boast about myself & I am not proud. I am not rude to people. I am not self-seeking in my relationships, easily angered by others, nor do I keep record of wrongs done to me. I do not side with evil but I rejoice when the truth is done. I always protect the other person, I always trust and believe the best of others. I always have hope that you have something good for them, and I always persevere in my relationships. I never fail to love others (1 Corinthians 13:4-8).

For as Jesus was, so am I in this world (1 John 4:17) and I am persuaded that you are love (1 John 4:16). I love as you love so that I may dwell in you, Father, and you in me (1 John4: 16) I love people and walk in the light and no stumbling befalls me (1 John 2:11). I love in deed and truth for it is pleasing in your sight (1 John 3:18, 22) and you have commanded me to love you and to love people as I love myself (Matt 22:39). I love for love is of you and because I am born of you and know you (1 John 4:7). I love you, Lord, because you first loved me and sent Jesus as atonement for my sins. I purposely love others that my love is made perfect that I may have boldness in the Day of Judgment.

I thank you that my countenance, my words, and my actions reflect the agapé love of Christ at all times, and that I see people as you see them and respond as you respond. I love and therefore have no fear, for perfect love casts out fear (1 John 4:18). I love you, Lord, and therefore I keep your commandments, which are not grievous to me. I love you and, being born of you, overcome the world, sin not, and the wicked one cannot touch me (1 John 5:3-4, 18). My love abounds more and more in understanding and expression so that I may sense, approve, and prize what is excellent and be blameless until the day of Christ (Philippians 1:9-10 AMP). I give thanks that you have granted me, according to your riches in glory, strength with might by your Spirit in my inner man. I have confidence that as Christ dwells in my heart; that I, being rooted and grounded in love, will be able to comprehend with all saints what is the breadth, and length, and depth, and height; and to know the love of Christ, which passes knowledge, that I may be filled with all the fullness of your Spirit (Eph 3:15-19). From this moment on, I walk in love and by your Spirit. I love according to your Word and I unconditionally accept your unconditional acceptance. In Jesus' name, Amen.

About the Author

Kelly Symone is a speaker, author, and passionate "Bible nerd." Whether serving through her local ministry or in business, Kelly leads with authenticity, strategic vision and uncommon insight to connect people to their highest purpose and performance. As founder of the Good Fruit Company, Kelly trains business and ministry leaders to embrace their God-given identities and transform culture by leaving a trail of good fruit behind them. She currently resides in the Chicago metropolitan area.

Visit her at <u>kellysymone.com</u>.